100 WALKS IN
NORTHERN ENGLAND

AA

Produced by AA Publishing
© AA Media Limited 2010

Published by AA Publishing (a trading name of AA Media Limited, whose registered office is Fanum House, Basing View, Basingstoke, Hampshire RG21 4EA; registered number 06112600)

This product includes mapping data licensed from Ordnance Survey® with the permission of the Controller of Her Majesty's Stationery Office.
© Crown copyright 2010. All rights reserved. Licence number 100021153

ISBN: 978-0-7495-6498-8
A04143

A CIP catalogue record for this book is available from the British Library.

The contents of this book are believed correct at the time of printing. Nevertheless, the publishers cannot be held responsible for any errors or omissions or for changes in the details given in this book or for the consequences of any reliance on the information it provides. We have tried to ensure accuracy, but things do change and we would be grateful if readers would advise us of any inaccuracies they encounter. This does not affect your statutory rights.

We have taken all reasonable steps to ensure that these walks are safe and achievable by walkers with a realistic level of fitness. However, all outdoor activities involve a degree of risk and the publishers accept no responsibility for any injuries caused to readers whilst following these walks. For more advice on using this book see page 11 and walking safely see page 112. The mileage range shown on the front cover is for guidance only – some walks may exceed or be less than these distances.

These routes appear in the AA Local Walks series and *1001 Walks in Britain*.

theAA.com/shop

Printed in China by Leo Paper Group

Picture credits
All images are held in the Automobile Association's own photo library (AA World Travel Library) and were taken by the following photographers:
Front cover S Day; 3 T Mackie; 6/7 T Mackie; 9 T Mackie; 10 P Sharpe.

Opposite: Swaledale, Yorkshire Dales National Park

Contents

Introduction and Locator Map 8
Using this Book 11

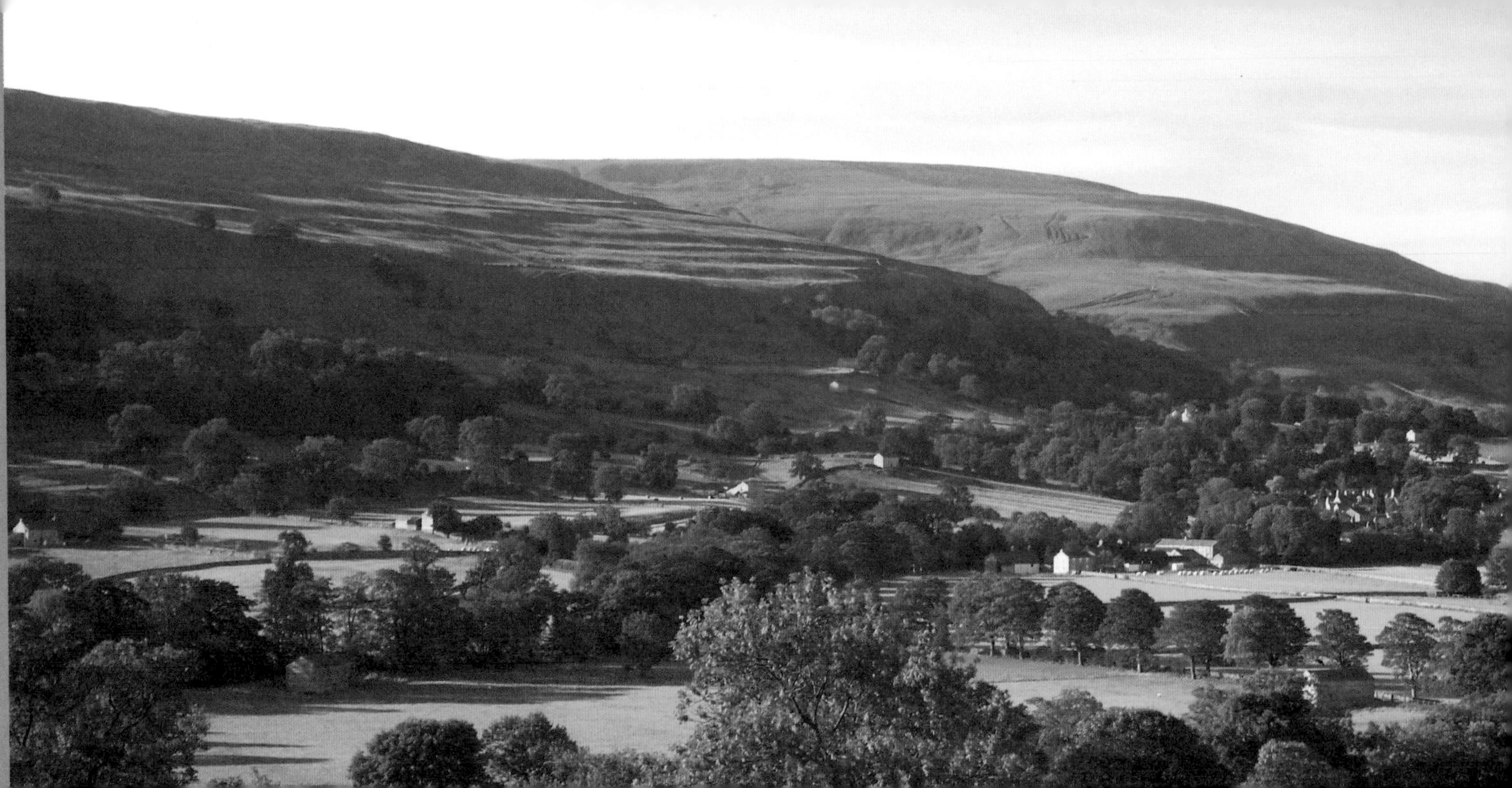

Northern England

This is a region of great industrial towns and cities, high moors and mountains, lakes and beautiful dales, and sweeping sands and wild shores. There is plenty of history, too, from the industry that shaped so much of the landscape to the great castles and monasteries that came before.

Northern England

This is walking country, which boasts five national parks: the Peak District, the Lake District, the North York Moors, the Yorkshire Dales and the Northumberland National Park. And down the centre, from Derbyshire to Scotland, runs the 256-mile (412km) Pennine Way.

From the Peak District National Park to the Lake District and the Scottish border, the northwest of England has mountains, lakes, and beautiful dales for the walker to discover. There are also lesser-known gems here – the high grouse moors of Bowland, the magical meandering Eden Valley, but this is also a region of historic cities – from ancient Chester to the Beatles' Liverpool. The hills dominate the northeast. The gritstone Pennines form a western boundary, only broken where the Tyne breaks through against the Scottish border. But there is also excellent walking along Yorkshire's heritage coast and on the wild Northumbrian shore.

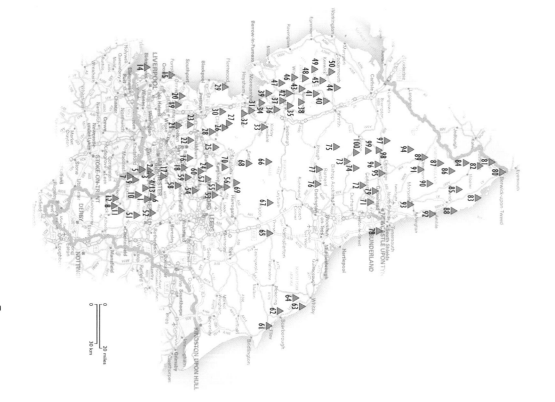

Bowland and the Cheshire Plain

Bowland Forest is a huge empty space of high moors and remote valleys. Below it the Lancashire plain is squeezed towards the sea. The Arnside and Silverdale Area of Outstanding Natural Beauty packs in a great deal of habitat diversity between the rivers Keer and Kent.

White Peak and Dark Peak

The White Peak is a limestone warren of dales and pretty stone villages. In the hills, you'll find nearly every valley has been flooded to quench the ceaseless metropolitan demand for water, which has created superb scenery. Hayfield and Ladybower are fine stretches of water surrounded by craggy hills.

Edale is the centrepiece of Derbyshire's Dark Peak. The pioneers of rambling started out from Chinley and Hayfield in the 1930s. And from Edale, the Pennine Way National Trail, the first long-distance footpath in Britain, begins its boggy journey northwards.

East of the Pennines

On the eastern slopes of the Pennines, West Yorkshire's towns and cities spill out over the eastern plains. To the south, Sheffield bites a share of this upland scenery, the millstone edges overlooking Derbyshire's dales. Yorkshire claims the lion's share of the Pennines. Here you will find the Three Peaks – Pen-y-ghent, Ingleborough and Whernside, as well as the Dales – Wharfedale, Swaledale, Wensleydale and a host of other valleys.

Moors and Hills

East of the Dales, across the Plain of York, the North York Moors and Howardian Hills rise up to meet the North Sea coast. The heather-topped moors seem to stop abruptly at the ocean – diving down in precipitous cliffs. Beyond these, and the great Tees river, industry has taken its toll. But at Marsden

Bay there is unsurpassed coastal scenery, then the Northumbrian coastline of beaches, dunes, castles and quiet inlets.

Lead mining dominated the North Pennines dales and the remains can be seen as you follow the rivers into Northumberland. Across the Tyne, and the Roman wall, the Cheviot Hills form an effective barrier against the Scots, and west of here the Border forest stretches into Cumbria.

Pennine Valleys

Bradfield is typical of many Pennine valleys – some have recovered better than others from the effects of industry. Striding across Rishworth Moor on the ancient trade route over Blackstone Edge you will feel remote. At Lydgate, ancient trackways take you high above the townscapes, and the sloping streets of Holmfirth will need no introduction to lovers of *Last of the Summer Wine*. From Wetherby

Pages 6–7: West Burton, Wensleydale, Yorkshire Dales National Park

Left: Swaledale, Yorkshire Dales National Park

to Addingham, there are many peaceful stretches of the River Wharfe to explore. Rising above, the slopes of Ilkley Moor inspired a Yorkshire anthem.

The Yorkshire Dales

The Yorkshire Dales proper start north of Ilkley and Skipton. The sight of Bolton Abbey's priory ruins by the River Wharfe will persuade you that you have left the cities behind. Nidderdale has reservoirs and limestone scenery, as well as the relics of lead mining, high on Greenhow Hill. The limestone theme is strongest in the western dales

and the waterfalls at Ingleton. North, at Ribblehead, you can see how the railway age tried to tame the wild landscape. The northern dales – Swaledale and Wensleydale – capture a special place in the hearts of all who visit them. The tiny village of Keld huddles on a hillside above the raging River Swale. Where the dale spills out into the Plain of York, Richmond and its castle stand guard. The River Ure runs through Wensleydale, an altogether more gentle affair.

The Lake District

The Lake District draws walkers and trippers alike for its sublime scenery. Windermere is England's largest lake, Wastwater its deepest. Scafell Pike is its highest mountain, Scale Force its tallest waterfall. The tourists flock to Coniston, Bowness and Keswick, but you can escape the crowds when you head further into the hills and dales. East of the Lakes, the River Eden has its origins high in the Yorkshire Dales, before winding beneath the highest of the Pennine fells to Carlisle, the Solway Firth and the border with Scotland. But those who make the journey over the Hartside Pass will be rewarded with a quiet, upland experience far

removed from the bustle of Dovedale or Tarn Hows.

To the Roman Wall

Weardale and the Derwent Valley have been heavily industrialised, but now forests clothe their lower reaches, in a tangle of river gorges and industrial archaeology. If you continue north you will reach Hadrian's Wall on the northern side of the Tyne Valley, now connected by a fine National Trail. While you're here, don't forget to visit the attractive towns of Hexham, with its great abbey church, and Morpeth with its river and 15th-century castle.

Northern National Park

Beyond the wall you are in the Northumberland National Park, a sparsely populated upland corner that stretches to the Cheviot Hills. Here you can explore the remote valleys of the upper Coquet and the Rede, the Breamish and the Till. On the northeast coast the great cliffs of Marsden Bay are worth exploring and no walker worth his salt should forgo the opportunity to wander around Lindisfarne.

Using this Book

❶ Information panels

Information panels show the total distance and total amount of ascent (that is the accumulated height you will ascend throughout the walk). An indication of the gradient you will encounter is shown by the rating 0–3. Zero indicates fairly flat ground and 3 indicates undulating terrain with several very steep slopes.

❷ Minimum time

The minimum time suggested is for approximate guidance only. It assumes reasonably fit walkers and doesn't allow for stops.

❸ Start points

The start of each walk is given as a six-figure grid reference prefixed by two letters indicating which 100km square of the National Grid it refers to. You'll find more information on understanding grid references on most Ordnance Survey maps.

❹ Abbreviations

Walk directions use these abbreviations:

L – left
L–H – left-hand
R – right
R–H – right-hand
Names which appear on signposts are given in brackets, for example ('Bantam Beach').

❺ Suggested maps

Details of appropriate maps are given for each walk, and usually refer to 1:25,000 scale Ordnance Survey Explorer maps. We strongly recommend that you always take the appropriate OS map with you. The maps in this book are there to give you the route and do not show all the details or relief that you will need to navigate around the routes provided in this collection. You can purchase Ordnance Survey Explorer maps at all good bookshops.

❻ Car parking

Many of the car parks suggested are public, but occasionally you may find you have to park on

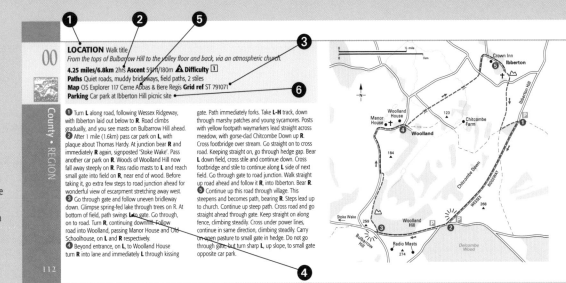

County · REGION

112

00

LOCATION Walk title
From the tops of Bulbarrow Hill to the valley floor and back, via an atmospheric church.

4.25 miles/6.8km 2hrs **Ascent** 591ft/180m ⛰ **Difficulty** ①
Paths Quiet roads, muddy bridleways, field paths, 2 stiles
Map OS Explorer 117 Cerne Abbas & Bere Regis **Grid ref** ST 791071
Parking Car park at Ibberton Hill picnic site

❶ Turn **L** along road, following Wessex Ridgeway, with Ibberton laid out below to **R**. Road climbs gradually, and you see masts on Bulbarrow Hill ahead. ❷ After 1 mile (1.6km) pass car park on **L**, with plaque about Thomas Hardy. At junction bear **R** and immediately **R** again, signposted 'Stoke Wake'. Pass another car park on **R**. Woods of Woolland Hill now fall away steeply on **R**. Pass radio masts to **L** and reach small gate into field on **R**, near end of wood. Before taking it, go extra few steps to road junction ahead for wonderful view of escarpment stretching away west. ❸ Go through gate and follow uneven bridleway down. Glimpse spring-fed lake through trees on R. At bottom of field, path swings **L** to gate. Go through, on to road. Turn **R**, continuing downhill. Follow road into Woolland, passing Manor House and Old Schoolhouse, on **L** and **R** respectively. ❹ Beyond entrance, on **L**, to Woolland House turn **R** into lane and immediately **L** through kissing

gate. Path immediately forks. Take **L-H** track, down through marshy patches and young sycamores. Posts with yellow footpath waymarkers lead straight across meadow, with gorse-clad Chitcombe Down up **R**. Cross footbridge over stream. Go straight on to cross road. Keeping straight on, go through hedge gap. Bear **L** down field, cross stile and continue down. Cross footbridge and stile to continue along **L** side of next field. Go through gate to road junction. Walk straight up road ahead and follow it **R**, into Ibberton. Bear **R**. ❺ Continue up this road through village. This steepens and becomes path, bearing **R**. Steps lead up to church. Continue up steep path. Cross road and go straight ahead through gate. Keep straight on along fence, climbing steadily. Cross under power lines, continue in same direction, climbing steadily. Carry on open pasture to small gate in hedge. Do not go through gate, but turn sharp **L**, up slope, to small gate opposite car park.

the roadside or in a lay-by. Please be considerate when you leave your car, ensuring that access roads or gates are not blocked and that other vehicles can pass safely. Remember that pub car

parks are private and should not be used unless you are visiting the pub or you have the landlord's permission to park there.

Opposite: Loweswater, Lake District National Park

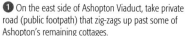

LADYBOWER RESERVOIR Lost Village

Beneath Ladybower Reservoir lies the remains of the old village of Ashopton.

5.5 miles/8.8km 3hrs 30min **Ascent** 1,200ft/365m ⚠ **Difficulty** ②
Paths Well-defined moorland paths and a reservoir road
Map OS Explorer OL1 Dark Peak **Grid ref** SK 195864
Parking Marked roadside parking bay east of Ashopton Viaduct

❶ On the east side of Ashopton Viaduct, take private road (public footpath) that zig-zags up past some of Ashopton's remaining cottages.

❷ Road becomes unsurfaced and gated, at edge of open country. Where road ends at turning point, double back **L** on forestry track climbing through pines and larches, signposted 'Whinstone Lee Tor'. Track emerges from shade of forest out on to Lead Hill, where Ladybower Reservoir and sombre sprawl of Bleaklow come into view.

❸ Path keeps intake wall to **L** as it rakes up bracken slopes of Lead Hill. Follow well-worn path away from wall up to ridge. At 6-way junction of tracks at top go 2nd **L** to reach Whinstone Lee Tor.

❹ Path continues along peaty ridge past Hurkling Stones to unnamed summit. Beyond this it meets

signposted path heading from Ladybower over to Moscar. Descend **L** until you reach gate at edge of open country.

❺ Through gate path descends westwards and alongside top wall of conifer plantation. It fords Grindle Clough's stream beyond another gate and turns **L** past several stone-built barns. Path, now paved, descends further to join track running along east shores of Ladybower Reservoir.

❻ It is worth doing detour here to see remains of Derwent village, which lies 400yds (366m) northwest along track at foot of Mill Brook clough. When you've seen old village, retrace steps along well-graded track, heading southwards along shores of reservoir. After rounding Grainfoot Clough track passes through woodland to return to Ashopton Viaduct.

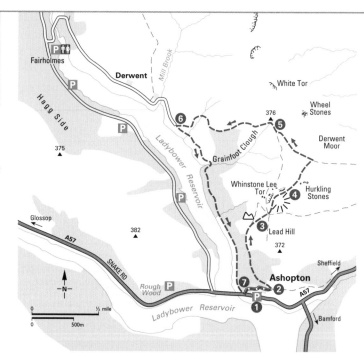

HAYFIELD On The Moorland's Edge

To Lantern Pike and Middle Moor.

7 miles/11.3km 4hrs **Ascent** 1,640ft/500m ⚠ **Difficulty** ☐2
Paths Good paths and tracks, plenty of stiles
Map OS Explorer OL1 Dark Peak **Grid ref** SK 036869
Parking Sett Valley Trail pay car park, Hayfield

1 Follow old railway trackbed signed 'The Sett Valley Trail and Pennine Bridleway', from car park in Hayfield west down valley and above River Sett to minor road close to A6015 New Mills road at Birch Vale.

2 Turn **R** along road, then **R** again along cobbled track behind cottages of Crescent into shade of woods. Beyond gate, track meets farm lane at hairpin bend. Follow higher course to reach country lane. Staggered to **R** across it, surfaced lane climbs further up hillside. Take **L** fork near Upper Cliffe Farm to gate at edge of National Trust's Lantern Pike site.

3 Leave bridleway here and turn **L** along grassy wallside path climbing heather and bracken slopes to rock-fringed ridge. Turn **R** and climb crest to Lantern Pike's summit, topped by view indicator.

4 From here, path continues north, descending to gate at northern boundary of National Trust estate, where it rejoins track you left earlier. Follow this north across high pastures to 5-way footpath signpost to west of Blackshaw Farm.

5 Turn **L** along walled farm lane past Bullshaw Farm, then **R** on track passing buildings of Matleymoor Farm. Where track swings **R** leave it for rough grassy track **L**. Cross stile at its end and continue north on grooved path, which joins semi-surfaced track from Knarrs.

6 At end turn **R** and walk along road to A624. Cross with care and go over stile at far side. Turn **R**, following faint, rutted track with wall on **R**. This crosses little valley of Hollingworth Clough on footbridge before climbing up heather slopes of Middle Moor.

7 Near white shooting cabin, turn **R** on stony Snake Path, which descends through heather, then, beyond kissing gate, across fields to reach walled track. Follow it to Kinder Road near centre of Hayfield.

8 Turn **R** down lane, then **L** down steps to Church Street. Turn **L** to St Matthew's Church, then **R** down side street signed 'Sett Valley Trail'. This leads to busy main road. Cross with care to car park.

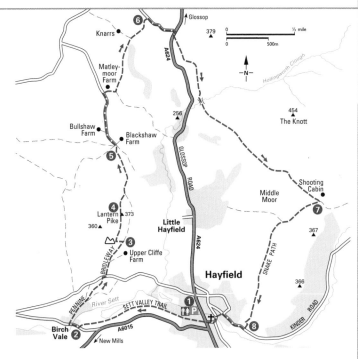

HAYFIELD The Trespass

A dramatic route to Kinder Downfall.

8 miles/12.9km 5hrs **Ascent** 1,450ft/440m ⚠ **Difficulty** ③
Paths Well-defined tracks and paths, quite a few stiles
Map OS Explorer OL1 Dark Peak **Grid ref** SK 048869
sParking Bowden Bridge pay car park

❶ Turn **L** out of car park and go up lane under trees and by banks of River Kinder. After 550yds (503m), leave lane at signposted footpath after crossing bridge. Follow path as it traces east bank of river; turn **L** to rejoin road just short of treatment plant buildings.
❷ Here fork **L** through gate on to cobbled bridleway, climbing above buildings. It continues alongside reservoir's north shore, turning sharp **L** on White Brow. Beyond gate, don't cross footbridge, follow path instead as it climbs alongside William Clough, where it is joined by Snake Path from **L**.
❸ Path crosses and recrosses stream as it works its way up grass and heather clough. In upper stages clough loses its vegetation and stream becomes trickle in peat. Climb to Ashop Head where you meet Pennine Way at crossroads of paths.
❹ Turn **R** to walk along slabbed Pennine Way path across moor towards Kinder Scout's northwest edge, then climb those last gritstone slopes on pitched

path to gain summit plateau. Now easy along edge.
❺ After turning **L** into rocky combe of River Kinder, Mermaid's Pool and Kinder Downfall (waterfalls) come into view. Descend to cross Kinder's shallow rocky channel about 100yds (91m) back from edge before turning **R** and continuing along edge.
❻ Beyond Red Brook, leave plateau by taking **R** fork, southwest, contouring round slopes under rocky edge.
❼ After passing The Three Knolls rocks and swinging **R** beneath slopes of Kinderlow End, go through gate in fence (grid reference 066867) before taking **R** fork to reach another gate in wall dividing moor and farmland. Go over stile next to it and then turn **L** through gateway. Descend trackless pastured spur, passing through gates and stiles at field boundaries to pass **L** of Tunstead Clough Farm.
❽ Turn **R** beyond farmhouse to follow track down into upper Sett Valley. At crossroads of lanes at bottom, go ahead along road to emerge at Bowden Bridge.

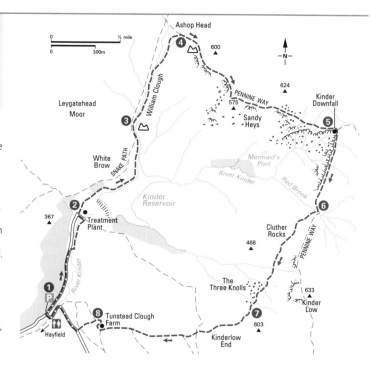

EDALE Ways On Kinder Scout

A walk along a section of the Pennine Way as it ascends to the craggy outcrops of the Kinder Plateau.

7 miles/11.3km 4hrs **Ascent** 1,650ft/500m ⚠ **Difficulty** ③
Paths Rock and peat paths, some steep ascents and descents
Map OS Explorer OL1 Dark Peak **Grid ref** SK 125853
Parking Edale pay car park

❶ Turn **R** out of car park and head north into Edale (village), under railway and past The Old Nags Head pub. By gate at far end turn **R** and then follow path across footbridge that leads over Grinds Brook.

❷ Leave main Grindsbrook Clough path by side of small barn, taking **R** fork that climbs up lower hillslope to reach stile on edge of open country. Beyond stile path zig-zags above Fred Heardman's Plantation then climbs up nose of The Nab to skyline rocks. Where path divides, take rather eroded **R** fork to summit of Ringing Roger.

❸ Follow edge path **L**, rounding cavernous hollow of Grindsbrook past Nether Tor. Old Pennine Way route is met on east side, at place marked by large cairn.

❹ Ignoring **L** fork heading for outlier of Grindslow Knoll, follow paved footpath westwards to head of another deep hollow, clough of Crowden Brook.

❺ Cross Crowden Brook, then leave edge to follow narrow level path traversing slopes on **L** beneath imposing outcrop of Crowden Tower. Below tower, turn **L** for steep, bumpy track down grassy hillside to brook. Keep to path that follows brook, fording it on several occasions.

❻ Go over stile at edge of open country, then cross footbridge shaded by tall rowans to change to west bank. From here path threads through woodland before descending in steps to road at Upper Booth. You now need to follow Pennine Way path back to Edale.

❼ Turn **L** along road and **L** again into farmyard of Upper Booth Farm before exiting at top **R** corner. After following track to gateway, bear **L** uphill to stile by old barn. Here Way traverses fields at foot of Broadlee Bank before joining tree-lined track into village. Tun **R** along road back to car park.

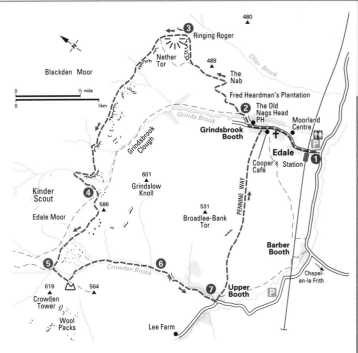

CHINLEY Edge Of The Moors
The green hills above Chinley.

5 miles/8km 3hrs **Ascent** 950ft/290m ⚠ **Difficulty** 2
Paths Field paths, quarry and farm tracks, a few stiles
Map OS Explorer OL1 Dark Peak **Grid ref** SK 041827
Parking Village car park on Station Road

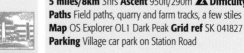

❶ Turn **L** on Green Lane, then **R** up Maynestone Road to pass war memorial. Leave road for signed path (grid ref 042828) through ginnel on **L**. Cross stile; climb northwest across fields towards Cracken Edge. At cart track turn **R**, then **L** on path passing between 2 hillside farmhouses. Go through gate past farm on **R** before climbing to lower edge of quarries.

❷ Swing **R** on sketchy path, passing hawthorn tree at base of hillslope. Join quarry track that zig-zags up slope then heads northwards beneath quarry cliffs. Go over stile in fence across track; climb by this fence to cliff top.

❸ Turn **R** along narrow edge path, then drop down to wall-walked lower path past quarried pits. Follow this over stile and continue beneath brow of hill and past Whiterakes cottage.

❹ Turn **R** on track from Hills Farm and drop to tarred lane which passes Peep-O-Day to A624.

❺ Cross and turn **L** along verge of busy road. After 150yds (137m) old cart track on **R** goes past small quarry. Turn **R** at T-junction of tracks to follow Pennine Bridleway across lower, grassy slopes of Mount Famine.

❻ It's worth making detour to visit top of South Head. Simply go through gate by National Trust sign and continue on track to summit. Resuming main route, go **R** over stile before gate and descend southwestwards to walled track.

❼ Follow this down to crossroads of routes north of Andrews Farm. Go straight on into field. Path soon develops into track and joins descending cart track from Andrews Farm.

❽ At A624 turn **R** for 50yds (46m) and then cross to signposted footpath, which cuts diagonally to **R** corner of 1st field before following wall towards Otter Brook. As old field boundary comes in from **R**, path turns half **L** to cross brook on slabbed bridge.

❾ Muddy path now climbs half **L** through scrubby woodland to Maynestone Road. Turn **L** and then follow road back to Chinley war memorial.

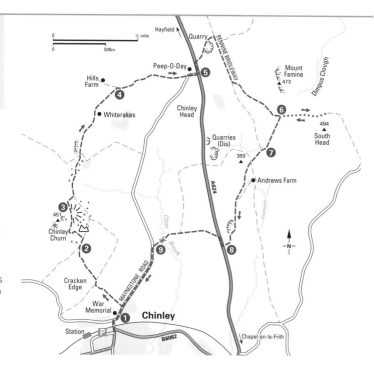

ALPORT CASTLES In The Clouds

Up to the rocky pinnacles of Alport Castles.

8 miles/12.9km 5hrs 30min **Ascent** 2,000ft/610m ⚠ **Difficulty** ③
Paths Well-defined paths and tracks in forests and on moorland
Map OS Explorer OL1 Dark Peak **Grid ref** SK 173893
Parking Fairholmes pay car park

❶ Leave car park for road, then follow forestry track, signposted 'Lockerbrook and Derwent Discovery Walk'. It climbs through Hagg Side Wood, crossing bridge over water leat before steepening on higher slopes. Near top waymarked path leaves forest in sight of farm.

❷ Obvious footpath, guided by stone wall, traverses fields of Lockerbrook Heights. Turn **L** at public footpath signpost and follow track southwards past Lockerbrook Farm.

❸ At ridgetop by Woodcock Coppice, turn **R** along permissive path climbing to open moor at Bellhag Tor.

❹ Continue over Rowlee Pasture and along ridgetop path climbing to Alport Castles.

❺ Descend on good path at southern end of Castles. Initially path follows old wall. On lower slopes it traces perimeter of Castles Wood.

❻ Cross footbridge over River Alport, where path turns **R**. Follow waymarks across field. At Alport Farm turn **L** on farm drive and then head southwards down valley.

❼ Where track veers **R** for Hayridge Farm, leave it

for signed path descending southeast towards edge of riverside wood, to exit on busy A57 Snake Road. Across road follow stony track to River Ashop, then cross footbridge to **R** of ford. Rejoin track, which skirts hillslopes beneath Upper Ashop Farm before climbing steadily across rough grassy slopes of Blackley Hey. Ignore **L** fork (surfaced drive) descending to Rowlee Bridge, but continue with track you're on as far as path intersection to east of Crookstone Barn.

❽ Turn **L** here on rutted track along top edge of pinewoods before entering them. Leave track just beyond **R-H** bend and follow narrow path to Haggwater Bridge.

❾ Beyond bridge, path climbs back up again to A57 Snake Road. Cross road and join track opposite. It climbs out of Woodlands Valley to east of Hagg Farm and zig-zags across upper slopes at edge of Woodcock Coppice before skirting Hagg Side conifer plantations. Here, retrace route down through Lockerbrook Coppice to car park.

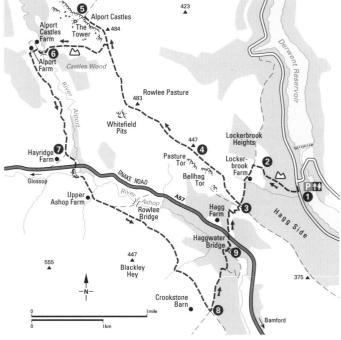

6

Derbyshire • NORTHERN ENGLAND

17

GOYT VALLEY Errwood Reservoir

Around Errwood Hall.

3.5 miles/5.7km 2hrs 30min **Ascent** 984ft/300m ⚠ **Difficulty** [1]
Paths Good paths and tracks, a few stiles
Map OS Explorer OL24 White Peak **Grid ref** SK 012748
Parking Errwood car park

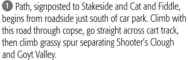

❶ Path, signposted to Stakeside and Cat and Fiddle, begins from roadside just south of car park. Climb with this road through copse, go straight across cart track, then climb grassy spur separating Shooter's Clough and Goyt Valley.

❷ Go through gate in wall on **R** that runs along spur and follow grassy path zig-zaging through woodland of Shooter's Clough before fording stream. Path heads north (**R**), through rhododendron bushes before continuing across open grassland to signposted footpath junction.

❸ Turn **R** here on good path skirting near side of wooded knoll, then ignoring 1st path through gateposts take 2nd **L** to Errwood Hall. Path continues past ruins, before descending steps to cross stream via footbridge.

❹ Climb steps on **R** to another footpath signpost. Turn **L** along path signposted to Pym Chair. This gradually swings north on hillslopes beneath Foxlow Edge. There's short detour down and **L** to see Spanish Shrine (visible from main path).

❺ 100yds (91m) on from Spanish Shrine, and before meeting road at top, path reaches open moorland. Take narrow path forking **R**, which climbs to top of Foxlow Edge. On reaching old quarry workings near top, path is joined by tumbledown dry-stone wall. Keep to narrow corridor between wall on **R** and the fence on **L**, ignoring little paths and tracks off **R** down into valley. Continue slow descent to far end of ridge.

❻ At fence corner, by edge of woodland follow path **L**, still downhill, around edge of trees and veer **L** again where it is joined by another path. With rhododendrons on **R**, follow broad, gravelly track down through woods to roadside at Shooter's Clough Bridge. Turn **R** and cross road bridge back to car park.

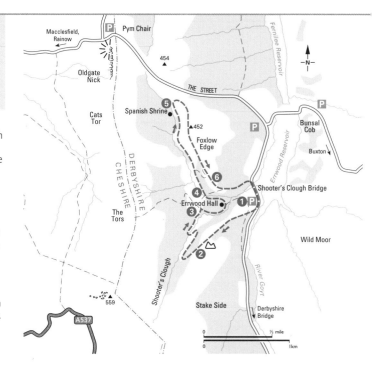

STANTON MOOR Sacred Worship

Circular walk across the mysterious Stanton Moor.

4 miles/6.4km 3hrs **Ascent** 540ft/165m ⚠ **Difficulty** 2
Paths Firm moorland tracks and field paths, a few stiles
Map OS Explorer OL24 White Peak **Grid ref** SJ 938697
Parking Roadside parking on Main Street, Birchover

❶ From Druid Inn at end of Main Street take signposted footpath on bend opposite. Follow this up along wooded ridge above village. Where it ends at quarry car park go **L** on to road. After 0.25 miles (400m) turn **R** for signposted path on to moor.
❷ Go over stile and veer **L** at Cork Stone for wide path across middle of heather moor. Stay on main path as it enters silver birch scrub, then swing **R** on wide grassy track, with fence over **L**, until you reach Nine Ladies.
❸ At Nine Ladies, walk to interpretation panel and turn **L** on main path. In 50 yds (46m) fork **R** for path through gorse and heather. Go over stile and turn **R** on to path along high wooded edge of moor to Earl Grey Tower. Continue on this open path to stile in fence on **R**.
❹ Cross over stile and at junction of tracks turn **L**. At crossroads of routes turn **L** again, downhill, to reach road. Turn **R** and walk along this for 50yds (46m) and

go **L** on footpath.
❺ Follow this well-signposted route along **L-H** edge of camping field, and then around buildings and ahead on rough farm track along **R-H** edge of 2 successive fields. When you meet unsurfaced Clough Lane turn **R**.
❻ Walk along lane to its end, at Cowley Knoll Farm. Turn **L** on to surfaced lane and almost immediately turn **R**, by Uppertown Farm, for gated path through fields. After hugging wall on **R** path continues past cottage and begins huge loop around hilly outcrop of Bradley Rocks. At far end go through gate to reach path junction.
❼ Ignore path downhill to **L** and continue with level track as it swings back east towards Birchover. Joining gravel drive on bend, take lower route and at crossroads of lanes go straight on past church to return to Birchover village and Main Street. To explore Rowtor Rocks look for narrow path on **L** just before Druid Inn.

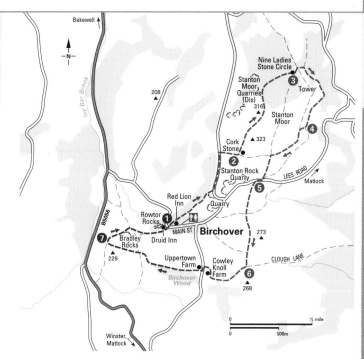

COMBS RESERVOIR A Quiet Corner
Around Combs Reservoir.

3 miles/4.8km 2hrs 30min **Ascent** 164ft/50m ⚠ **Difficulty** ☐1

Paths Can be muddy, quite a few stiles
Map OS Explorer OL24 White Peak **Grid ref** SK 033797 **Parking** Combs reservoir car park

❶ Follow path from dam along reservoir's western shore, ignoring 1st footbridge over Meveril Brook.

❷ As reservoir narrows path traverses fields, then comes to another footbridge over brook. This time cross it and head south to continue across another field. Beyond foot tunnel under Buxton line railway, path reaches hedge-lined country lane. Turn **L** along lane and continue into Combs village.

❸ Past Beehive Inn in village centre, take lane straight ahead, then **L** fork, signposted to Dove Holes. This climbs out of village towards Combs Edge.

❹ Take 2nd footpath on **L**, which begins at muddy clearing just beyond Millway Cottage. Go through stile and climb on partially slabbed path and then uphill across pasture with wall on **R**. Away **R** is huge comb of Pyegreave Brook. Climb pathless spur and go through gateways in next 2 boundary walls before following wall on **R**. Ignore gate in this wall – path to Bank Hall Farm – but stay with narrow path raking across rough grassy hillslopes with railway line and the reservoir below **L**.

❺ Path comes down to track that runs alongside railway line. This joins lane just short of Lodge. Turn **L** to go under railway and north to Down Lee Farm.

❻ Turn **L** through kissing gate 200yds (183m) beyond farmhouse. Signposted path follows overgrown hedge towards Marsh Hall Farm. Fields can become very boggy on final approaches. At farm complex turn **R** over stile and then follow vehicle track heading in northwesterly direction.

❼ After 200yds (183m) turn **L** on field path that heads west to stile at edge of Chapel-en-le-Frith golf course. Waymark arrows show way across fairway. Stile marking exit from golf course is 300yds (274m) short of clubhouse. You then cross small field to B5470.

❽ Turn **L** to walk along road (there's pavement on far side), and follow it past Hanging Gate pub at Cockyard. After passing sailing club entrance, turn **L** to cross dam of Combs Reservoir and continue ahead to return to car park.

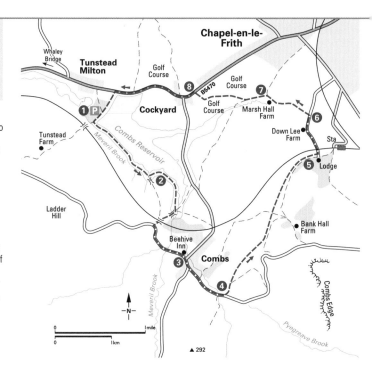

CASTLETON Castles And Caverns

Where the White and Dark peaks collide.

5 miles/8km 3hrs **Ascent** 820ft/250m ⚠ **Difficulty** ☐1

Paths Path below Blue John Mines can be tricky in wintry conditions
Map OS Explorer OL1 Dark Peak **Grid ref** SK 149829
Parking Main Castleton pay car park by visitor centre

❶ Turn **L**; go down main street; turn **R** along Castle Street, passing church and youth hostel on your way.
❷ At Market Place, turn **L** to Bar Gate, where signpost points to Cave Dale. Through gate, path enters limestone gorge with ruined keep of Peveril Castle perched on cliffs to **R**.
❸ As you gain height gorge shallows. Go through gate in dry-stone wall and follow well-defined track across high pastureland. It passes through gate in another wall before being joined by path that has descended hillside on **R**. Track divides soon after junction. Take **L** fork, which climbs uphill, slightly away from wall on **R**, to top corner of field. Go through gate here and follow short stretch of walled track to crossroads of routes near old Hazard Mine.
❹ Turn **R** beyond gate here to walk along stony walled lane, which swings **R** to minor road near Oxlow House Farm. Take path across road to disused quarry on Windy Knoll.

❺ At quarry turn **R** on grassy footpath to minor road. After turning **L** to next junction, take old Mam Tor Road (straight ahead).
❻ After 400yds (366m) turn **R** down approach road to Blue John Cavern, then **L** by ticket office. Enter gate and trace path as it crosses fields. Beyond gate path arcs **R**, traversing now steep grassy hillslopes. It passes Treak Cliff Cavern ticket office. Go **L** down steps by ticket office, then **R** on a path with handrails.
❼ Half-way down steps, take hillside path on **R**, signposted 'Winnats Pass'. On approach to Speedwell Cavern path becomes indistinct, but obvious stile ahead will take you out on to Winnats road.
❽ Path on far side of road takes route through National Trust's Longcliff Estate. It roughly follows line of wall and veers **L** beneath hill slopes of Cow Low to reach Goosehill Hall. Here, follow Goosehill (lane), back into Castleton. Beyond Goosehill Bridge, turn **L** down surfaced streamside path to car park.

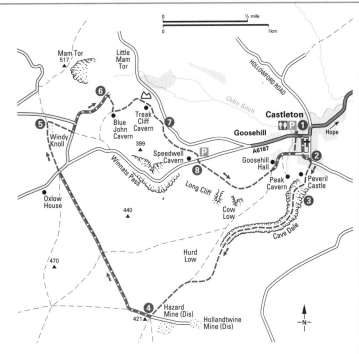

CHATSWORTH Park And Gardens

Past gardens and through parkland created by gardening guru, 'Capability' Brown.

7 miles/11.3km 3hrs 30min **Ascent** 459ft/140m ⚠ **Difficulty** ①
Paths Good paths and forest trails
Map OS Explorer OL24 White Peak **Grid ref** SK 251699
Parking Endensor village

❶ From Edensor village cross B6012 and take footpath at **R-H** side of large tree. Walk across parkland to join main drive to Chatsworth House. Just before bridge, cross the road and walk downhill to riverbank.

❷ Follow River Derwent past 2 weirs and remains of old mill to next bridge that carries B6012 over river. To **L** of bridge metal kissing gate allows access to road. Cross bridge.

❸ Ignore **L** turn into drive past gatehouse to estate but take next immediate **L** alongside gatehouse and continue uphill, past house on **R** and then farm, and cross stile on **L**.

❹ Cross field, go over next stile and then go diagonally **L**, uphill following waymarkers on well-defined path. When this meets broad track at top go **L**, cross wall into estate by high stile and continue to crossroads.

❺ Go ahead and follow track as it passes Swiss Lake on **R** and then loops round Emperor Lake on **L**. At crossroads with tarmac lane turn **L** for Hunting Tower.

❻ Continue on tarmac track as it loops **L** around tower, ignoring turning **R**. It heads downhill, past what appears to be remains of old viaduct with water cascading from end, then doubles back, still going downhill eventually reaching car park at Chatsworth House.

❼ Go past wooden hut at car park entrance and turn **R** on to estate road heading north. Follow this past wooden sculptures until you are within sight of gates at end of estate.

❽ Near here turn **L** across park to gate that leads eventually to Baslow. Don't go through gate but turn **L** on to trail that follows river back to Chatsworth. Turn **R** on to road, cross bridge then go immediately **R** on track which leads back to start in Edensor village.

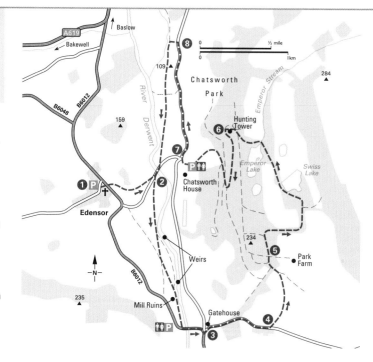

ARBOR LOW Ancient Circles

Around Arbor Low – the 'Stonehenge of the North' and an ancient trade centre.

6 miles/9.7km 4hrs **Ascent** 492ft/150m ⚠ **Difficulty** 2
Paths Mostly well-defined paths, some road walking; limestone steps in Cales Dales can be very slippery when wet; several stiles
Map OS Explorer OL24 White Peak **Grid ref** SK 194645 **Parking** Moor Lane pay car park

1 Exit car park on Moor Lane, turn **L** then follow road to Y-junction. Cross road, go through wall gap, through kissing gate and follow well-defined path across field.

2 Cross 2 wall stiles and continue on path. Cross fence by another stile and continue to wall at edge of wood. Go through kissing gate into Low Moor Wood.

3 Follow path through wood, go through gate and follow well-defined path across another field. Take diverted path round Calling Low Farm via 2 kissing gates, go through wood and 3 more kissing gates to get back on to open meadow.

4 Follow this path diagonally downhill and then go through more kissing gates. Continue on path still downhill, through another gate into Lathkill Dale National Nature Reserve. Head downhill on limestone path and steps. Cross stile at bottom and then head uphill on path to **L**.

5 Look out for cave in rocks on **L** as you reach top. Continue uphill, through gate and on to farm. Enter farm steading via stone steps and continue on road, uphill between buildings until you see signpost for Cales Farm pointing **L**.

6 Turn on to this farm road and follow it to main road. Turn **R** and continue for 0.5 mile (800m) then turn **L** on to drive for Upper Oldhams Farm, following signs for henge.

7 Go through farm yard following signs, go through gate, turn **L** along path then cross another stile to reach henge. Retrace steps to main road, turn **R** and walk about 2.5 miles (4km) back to car park.

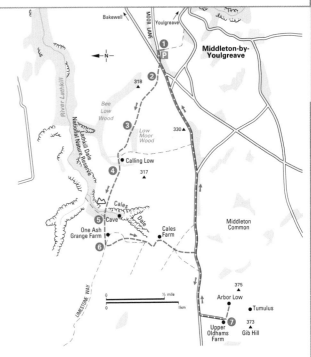

EDALE Mysterious Mam Tor

Approaching from the Edale side, discover the ancient secrets of the great 'Shivering Mountain'.

6 miles/9.7km 3hrs 30min **Ascent** 984ft/300m ⚠ **Difficulty** ②
Paths Mainly good but can be boggy in wet weather
Map OS Explorer OL1 Dark Peak **Grid ref** SK 124853
Parking Edale pay car park

❶ Exit car park at Edale and turn **R** on to main road. Look out for public footpath sign on **L** and turn on to farm road. Just before road turns sharply **L**, take public footpath that forks off **R** and goes uphill through wood.

❷ At end of wooded area cross stile and then continue walking uphill. Go across another stile, follow path across open hillside, then cross yet another stile and turn **L** on to road. Just before road bends sharply **L**, cross road, go over stile and follow path towards hill.

❸ Near foot of hill cross stile to **L** and turn **R** on to road. Continue to find steps on **L** leading through Iron Age fort ramparts to summit of Mam Tor. From here trace your steps back to road.

❹ Cross road, go over stile and continue on footpath uphill and on to Rushup Edge. Follow this well-defined path along ridge crossing 5 stiles. When path is intersected by another, go **R**. This is Chapel Gate track, badly eroded in places.

❺ Near hill bottom go through gap stile on **L**. Go across another stile, then through gate and across yet another stile on **L**. This leads to tumbledown buildings. Cross stile by corner of 1 building and then veer **R** to cross another stile on to farm road.

❻ Cross road, go through gate and then follow path until it joins road. Turn **R** and then **L** at junction and into Barber Booth. Take 2nd turn on **L** on tarmac lane, then, near village outskirts, turn **L** on road signposted to Edale Station.

❼ Follow path across fields, forking **R** after Shaw Wood Farm. Finally emerge on road next to Champion House. Turn **L** to visit Moorland Centre, (100yds/91m) right to car park.

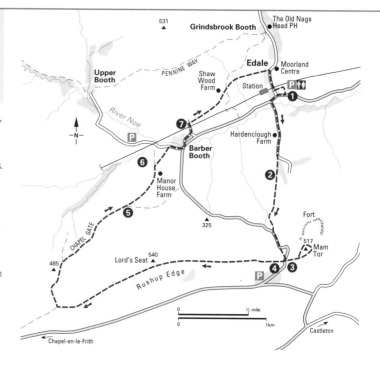

THURSTASTON Uncommon Delights

Panoramic views from a heathland crest.

5.25 miles/8.4km 1hr 45min **Ascent** 345ft/105m ⚠ **Difficulty** 1
Paths Some road walking, sandy tracks and bare rock, then field paths, 2 stiles
Map OS Explorer 266 Wirral & Chester **Grid ref** SJ 238834
Parking Wirral Country Park at bottom of Station Road, Thurstaston

1 From car park, loop round past visitor centre and wildlife pond, go out to Station Road and straight up for 0.5 mile (800m). At top it swings **R**.

2 Turn **L** before church and go up to A540. Go **L**, past Cottage Loaf, then **R** through kissing gate. Follow track ahead past school to end of cul-de-sac.

3 Go through kissing gate to broad path then go **R** on smaller path. Cross track near cattle grid then beyond wide gate swing **L** to join another track. This keeps just inside edge of wood, following course of Greasby Brook.

4 A boundary wall appears ahead. Turn **L** alongside it. Where it ends keep ahead, passing model railway. Alongside Royden Park wall resumes, where it ends turn **L** by sign and map. Cross clearing to junction.

5 20yds (18m) further on is kissing gate. Turn **R** before it, on narrow path. At T-junction turn **R**, then at end of this go **L** on broader path. Beyond marker stone continue over tree roots and bare rock, then at

junction of paths among light woodland and with drop ahead go **L**. Follow wide and soon open edge of rocky escarpment up to sandstone pillar with map/view indicator and then trig point. Continue short distance to end of ridge and take **L** fork. Descend broad path that rejoins outward route. Retrace steps past Cottage Loaf and down top section of Station Road.

6 Turn **L** past church. When road swings round **L**, lane continues ahead. Cross stile and follow well-marked footpath. In dip cross stream and turn **R** at footpath sign. After recrossing stream, zig-zag down steeper slope into The Dungeon.

7 Cross stream again and follow it down. Climb on to old railway embankment and go **R**. When green gates bar route, sidestep **L**. Continue for another 220yds (201m) to hedge gap. Follow path, winding past 2 ponds then out to cliff tops above estuary. Go **R** for 240yds (219m), then bear **R** across grass towards visitor centre and car park.

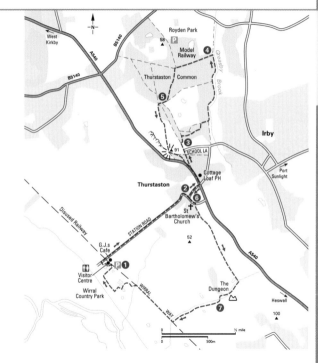

FORMBY POINT Squirrels And Sand

An exhilarating walk through an area of great significance for wildlife.

3.5 miles/5.7km 1hr 30min **Ascent** 50ft/15m ⚠ **Difficulty** ☐

Paths Well-worn paths through woods and salt marsh, plus long stretch of sand
Map OS Explorer 285 Southport & Chorley **Grid ref** SD 278082
Parking Either side of access road just beyond kiosk

❶ Start just **L** of large notice board. Follow 'Squirrel Walk', with its wooden fencing, to **L** and then round to **R**. Keep straight on at several crossroads. There are many subsidiary paths but main line runs virtually straight to Blundell Avenue. Cross avenue to fainter path almost opposite, with 'No Cycling' sign and traces of bricks in its surface. Follow this, skirting around field edge (brick traces are still useful guide). Go up slight rise then across more open sand hills to pines on rise ahead. Skirt **L** round hollow and see houses on edge of Formby ahead.

❷ Just before reaching houses turn **R** on straight track. This swings **L** slightly then forks. Go **R**, down steps, then straight on alongside reed-fringed pool. Go straight on, over crossroads towards sand hills. When you reach them swing **L** then **R**, picking up boardwalk, to skirt highest dunes and out to beach.

❸ Turn **R** along open and virtually level sand. Walk parallel to dunes (heading north) for over 1.25 miles (2km). Shoreline curves gently to **R** but there are f ew distinctive landmarks apart from yellow-topped signs to approach paths. Watch for sign for Gipsy Wood Path.

❹ Distinct track winds through sand hills then swings more decisively **R** near pools, where there's sign board about natterjack toads. Follow track back into woods and, at junction, go **R**. Route curves round between woods and sand hills then joins wider track by Sefton Coastal Footpath sign. Go **R** through willows then bear **L** to pines on rise. From these drop to broad path with gravelly surface and follow it **L** into woods again. Stick to main path, with timber edgings and white-topped posts, bear **R** by large 'xylophone', and continue quickly back to start.

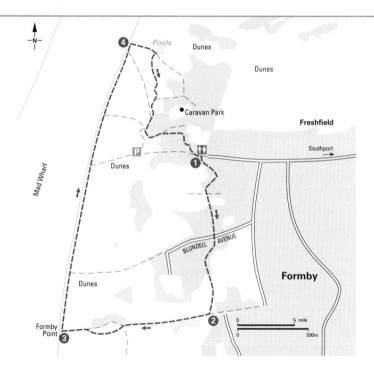

HEALEY DELL A Hidden Gem

Around a gem of a nature reserve.

2.5 miles/4km 1hr **Ascent** 640ft/195m △ **Difficulty** [2]
Paths Field paths, old railway line and surfaced tracks, 5 stiles
Map OS Explorer OL21 South Pennines **Grid ref** SD 879155
Parking By Healey Dell Nature Reserve Visitor Centre

❶ With your back to visitor centre, turn **L** and walk past first range of buildings. Cross gated bridge and turn **R**. Take lower path, along river, past more overgrown ruins. Near green footbridge go sharp **L** up bank then **R**, along edge of clearing, and back into woods. Go **L**, just before stream, on narrow path, climbing steeply in places. Stone flags help over wet patch before path dips to cross stream. Climb again on other side and join broader green track. Where this narrows, go over stile and up field edge to Smallshaw Farm.

❷ Go **L** before 1st building then through gate into the yard. Go **L** on track to road. Go **R** and up to bus turning circle. Turn **R** opposite this along track. Follow this for 400yds (366m) to Knack's Farm.

❸ Continue over cattle grid and down lane, then fork **R** on track. After slight dog-leg track becomes greener. Follow it round **L** and back **R**, then over stile ahead and down field by fence and ruined wall. Go over stile at the bottom, down to lane and go **L** few paces.

❹ Go down ramp and steps to old railway line. Turn **R** along it for 500yds (457m) then cross viaduct high above Dell. Go **L** down steps to access lane, under viaduct then sharply back **R** on broad path. Where this starts to level out there's 4-bar stile on **L**. But first walk short way upstream to see cascades.

❺ Return to stile and cross it. Follow stone setts (often slippery) down to sharp bend, with more remains just down and **R**. From bend footpath follows tops of old walls then curls down steeply to weir. Step across water-cut on stone slabs and follow it down. When it enters tunnel carved in solid rock, footpath goes to **R**. Almost opposite tall pillar it swings away from river and out past terrace of houses to lane. Go down this below tall brick retaining wall and back to start.

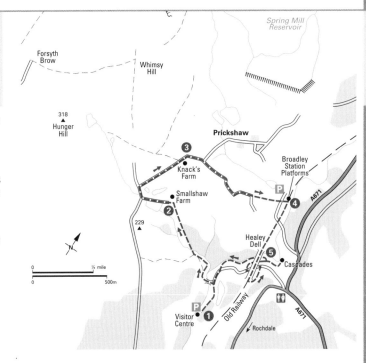

DOVE STONES Another Peak Experience
Along the edge of the moors.

8 miles/12.9km 3hrs **Ascent** 1,296ft/395m △ **Difficulty** 3
Paths Mostly on good tracks but with some rocky sections, occasionally very steep, 2 stiles
Map OS Explorer OL1 Dark Peak **Grid ref** SE 013034
Parking Dovestone Reservoir, pay at weekends

❶ From car park walk to top of Dovestone Reservoir dam and turn **R**, along road past sailing club. Where plantation ends go over bridge and straight on to follow private, vehicular track as it makes its way steadily to top of Chew Valley.

❷ At Chew Reservoir turn **L** and walk along by dam wall until just before it kinks **R**. With your back to reservoir (and near sign warning of deep water) drop down to moorland and follow wide, straight track opposite that heads back towards edge of hillside. It first bears **L**, then swings back to **R**, and soon becomes thin path that weaves its way between loose rocks around Dish Stone Brow.

❸ With Dovestone Reservoir coming into view below, continue along high rim of hillside past rocky outcrops. If you occasionally lose sight of path, just keep to wide strip between steep drop on **L** and banks of peaty bog on **R**.

❹ Nearing Great Dove Stone Rocks continue to

follow rocky edge as it swings back to **R**. Beyond Dean Rocks clear path winds its way around head of narrow valley known as Dove Stone Clough.

❺ Cross stream as it flows over rocky shelf and, as you continue across slope on far side, narrow path slowly begins to drop down grassy hillside. Fork **L** and ignore higher path towards prominent stone memorial cross ahead. Soon path curves steeply down to **L** and there are numerous criss-crossing tracks through long grass and bracken. If in doubt just aim for unmistakable aqueduct below you, at foot of Dove Stone Clough, and cross it by high footbridge.

❻ Walk along path below rock face and fence on **L** and across slumped hillside littered with rock debris. Eventually path joins grassy strip that gently leads down between fenced-off conifer plantations. Go through gate and drop down through open field to reach popular reservoir-side track. Turn **L** and then follow this track back to car park.

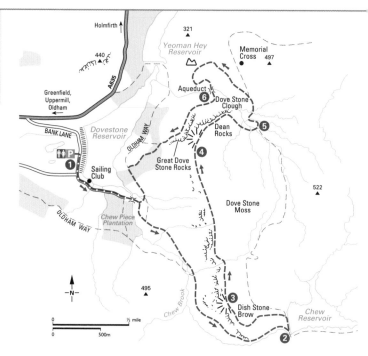

BLACKSTONE EDGE Roman Ways

A steady climb to a rocky ridge.

6.5 miles/10.4km 2hrs 30min **Ascent** 1,066ft/325m ⚠️ **Difficulty** ③
Paths Field paths, rough tracks and faint paths across open moorland, 2 stiles
Map OS Explorer OL21 South Pennines **Grid ref** SD 940153
Parking Hollingworth Lake Visitor Centre pay car park

❶ From far end of car park path runs past picnic tables then crosses and follows small beck. At track go left 200yds (183m) then **R** with yellow arrows. Zig-zag up slope then **L** and down to stream and footbridge. Where path forks keep to lower one, just above stream. It wriggles through woods then up to wider path and round to Owlet Hall.

❷ Go through wooden gate and **L** alongside house to stile. Cross stream, and then stile. Ignore path on **L** and keep **R**, just above stream, along line of thorn trees. Cross decrepit fence and follow neglected path alongside wall. Go up to trees flanking drive to Shore Lane Farm. Turn **L**, then **L** again on lane.

❸ Just before road, turn **R** on track to walk past houses. Continue on narrower but clear path. Meet farm track just below A58, go **R** for few paces, then **L** up well-worn path, former Roman road. Cross water-cut and keep climbing. Slope eases near Aggin Stone.

❹ Turn **R**, through kissing gate and follow rough path across rock-strewn moor to trig point. Follow main edge south for 400yds (366m) to break in line of rocks.

❺ Slant down **R** across rough moor to old water-cut. Go **L** alongside this until path veers **R**. Path soon rises again, across shoulder of moor, then levels off by small cairn. Keep **R**, along edge, descend more steeply then swing **R**, joining old grooved track. Continue down green track, past cairn, then back **L** descending towards Dry Mere.

❻ Where ground steepens, just beyond tarn, path splits. Take lower one, towards pylon. Go across well-used track to another track below. Go **L**, fording small stream, then swing **R**. Drop down to shale track in valley and go **R** down it.

❼ At Syke farm join surfaced lane. At Hollingworth Fold, with its multicoloured signpost, keep ahead down lane to join lakeside road. Entrance to visitor centre is just across 1st embankment.

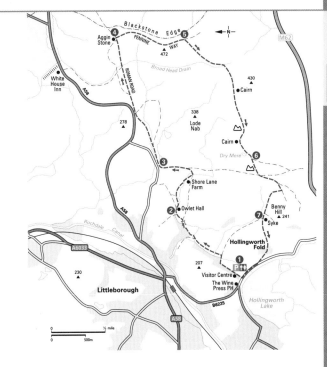

RIVER DOUGLAS Valley Delights

A gentle yet surprising corner of Lancashire.

4 miles/6.4km 1hr 45min **Ascent** 410ft/125m ⚠ **Difficulty** 2
Paths Field paths and canal towpath, 11 stiles
Map OS Explorer 285 Southport & Chorley **Grid ref** SD 517109
Parking Large lay-by on A5209

1 At end of lay-by cross stile into field corner. Go up field edge and **L** along field top, then into wood. Cross footbridges and continue up footpath, then alongside stream. Follow side of conifer plantation until it bends away, then bear **R** to **L-H** side of trees enclosing pool. Continue up to **R** into enclosed track below power lines and on up to junction with tarmac track.

2 Go **L**, then bear **L** again down earthy track. At end of track go straight ahead on fenced path between fields, to corner of wood, over stile and then down its **L-H** edge. Keep following this, which eventually becomes strip of woodland, to stile in bottom corner of field. Follow footpath down through wood then up to A5209.

3 Cross road and go **L** to stile where pavement ends. Go straight down field and over another stile into lane. Go **R** then immediately **L** down another lane. Cross railway at level crossing and continue until to bridge over canal. Drop to towpath and follow it **L**

(eastwards) for 0.5 mile (800m) to next canal bridge (No 40).

4 Cross this bridge and follow obvious track, taking you back over railway and up to junction of tracks. Turn **R**, on track past houses, then follow waymarks for narrower path alongside private track. Where this ends at stile, keep ahead across open field aiming for post and stile into woodland.

5 Descend steep steps into wood and then bear **L** into Fairy Glen. Cross footbridge, climb steps, then go **L** up good track. Cross another footbridge below waterfall and ascend more steps. Keep to principal footpath, straight on up glen as it becomes shallower, until path crosses tiny footbridge. Soon after, footpath leaves side of brook and briefly joins track before it emerges on to A5209. Cross and go **R**, back to reach lay-by at start.

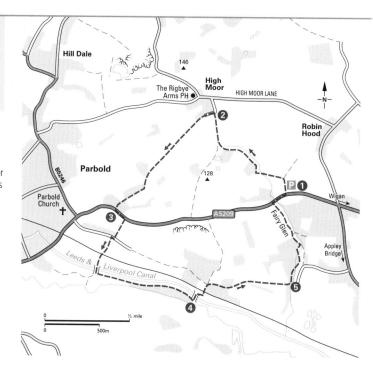

MARTIN MERE Lancashire 'Fens'

An easy walk around a superb bird centre.

5 miles/8km 2hrs **Ascent** 50ft/15m ⚠ **Difficulty** ☐1
Paths Canal towpaths, lanes, farm tracks and field paths, 4 stiles
Map OS Explorer 285 Southport & Chorley **Grid ref** SD 423126
Parking Several small lay-bys near mid-point of Gorst Lane

❶ Near mid-point of Gorst Lane follow short track up through small timber yard to meet canal by old swing bridge. Go **R** along towpath for about 0.75 mile (1.2km) to Gregson's Bridge. Go under bridge then continue up to lane.

❷ Go **L** and join wider road (Martin Lane); follow it away from canal for about 350yds (320m). At bend, by Martin Inn, bear **R** down narrow lane. Follow this for about 700yds (640m), past tea rooms at 'The Farm, Burscough', to very open section. Opposite glasshouses there's footpath sign **R**. Follow track to railway line.

❸ Cross line and continue down track to green shed. Go **R**, alongside drainage ditch, until another ditch appears ahead. From here go **R** and then **L** on waymarked concessionary route around edge of Martin Mere Reserve. This clear and easy track that has viewing position into heart of reserve. Keep to outer edge of embankment and eventually swing **L**. Beyond gate follow edge of high, straight fence to road.

(Turn **L** here to reach reserve's main entrance, about 400yds/366m along.)

❹ Turn **R** and follow road for 500yds (457m). About 100yds (91m) past Brandreth Barn you see footpath sign on **R**. Go along this to large shed and turn **L**, past pool, and on down obvious track across open fields.

❺ At end of track, just before lane, turn **R** on concrete track. Then, turn **R** before house and follow fence round **L**. Keep almost straight on ignoring signpost pointing **R**, and cross field straight ahead aiming towards 2 trees. These act as direction posts down field edges to railway line. Cross and keep straight on, following slightly raised line of old field boundaries, then join track to, and then through Crabtree Bridge Farm.

❻ Swing **R** on towpath. It's about 200yds (183m) to swing bridge by The Farmers Arms and another 500yds (457m) to smaller one above timber yard. Drop back down through this to Gorst Lane.

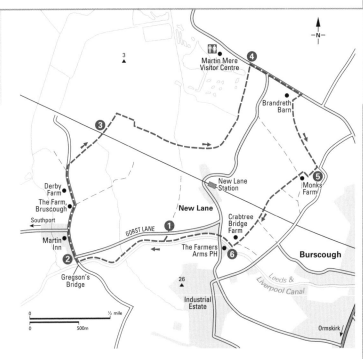

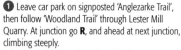

ANGLEZARKE Rocks And Water

Walking in a landscape shaped by reservoirs and quarries.

7.25 miles/11.7km 2hrs 45min **Ascent** 689ft/210m ⚠ **Difficulty** 2
Paths Mostly good tracks with some field paths, 16 stiles
Map OS Explorer 287 West Pennine Moors **Grid ref** SD 621161
Parking Large car park at Anglezarke

❶ Leave car park on signposted 'Anglezarke Trail', then follow 'Woodland Trail' through Lester Mill Quarry. At junction go **R**, and ahead at next junction, climbing steeply.

2 Go through gap on **L**, on bend. Path traverses wooded slope. Descend steps, join wider track and go **L**. Beyond kissing gate narrower path to road.

❸ Go **L** 50yds (46m) to kissing gate. Follow track up valley below Stronstrey Bank. Cross bridge then go through kissing gate to White Coppice cricket ground.

❹ Bear **L** up lane, then follow tarmac into White Coppice hamlet. Cross footbridge by post box. Follow stream and then go up **L** by a reservoir. Bear **L** to stile. Cross next field to its top **R** corner and then go **R** on lane. Where it bends **R** go **L** up track.

❺ Skirt Higher Healey, follow field edges, then angle up **L** into dark plantations. Fork **L** just inside, and ascend to old quarry entrance. Keep **L** on main path around it, drop down through woods and up to gate.

Go **R** at crossroads and up woodland edge.

❻ At top turn **L** for large cairn on Grey Heights. Descend to **R** on path, near wall, and at junction go **L**, over stile. Eventually track leads to White House farm.

❼ Cross stile on **L**, below farmyard wall, then bear **L** to field corner. Cross stile on **L** then up field edge and join confined, fenced path. From stile on **R** follow trees along field edge to rough track. Go **R** and straight on to Kays Farm.

❽ Go **R** on track then **L** on lane below reservoir wall. As lane angles away, go **L** over stile then skirt reservoir until pushed away from water by wood. Join road across dam. Go through gap and up steep track. Go **L** at top round Yarrow Reservoir to road.

❾ Go **L**, passing entrance to Anglezarke Quarry, to junction. Go **R**, and car park entrance is on 1st bend.

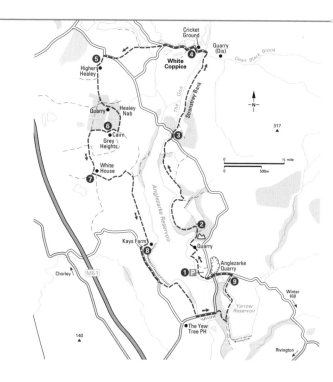

HASLINGDEN GRANE The Deserted Village

A walk that lays bare the past.

3.5 miles/5.7km 1hrs 30min **Ascent** 426ft/130m ⚠ **Difficulty** 2
Paths Good tracks, a few steep and rough sections, 5 stiles
Map OS Explorer 287 West Pennine Moors **Grid ref** SD 752232
Parking At Clough Head Information Centre car park (locked 5pm), B6232

❶ Footpath starts immediately **L** of information centre. Go through plantation then climb alongside wall. Go through kissing gate by Rossendale Way sign then go immediately **L** over stone slab stile and follow almost level path along fine wall. After 100yds (91m) past plantation, go **L** over stile by Rossendale Way sign and down to road.

❷ Go **L** down road for 90yds (82m), then **R** on track, swinging **R** to pass ruins. After about 440yds (402m) track swings **L** again near spoil heaps. Stay on this past more ruins, then dip into valley alongside old water-cut.

❸ At end go **R** 50yds (46m) on walled track, then **L** again across short wet patch. Follow old walled track past ruined houses and into another valley, just above extensive ruins. Skirt **R** round these and descend to stream then climb up alongside plantation. Cross into this at kissing gate. Path starts level but soon descends quite steeply, winding past Rossendale Way signs, to meet clearer path at bottom.

❹ Turn **R**, cross footbridge and go up steps then across hillside below beech wood. Cross small stream, go up few paces then go **L** and follow generally level path. Continue along bilberry-covered hillside above Calf Hey Reservoir, passing ruin on **L** and through dip containing stream. Another 90yds (82m) further, large sycamore tree stands on its own.

❺ Go through kissing gate just below tree then descend slightly **R** to stile by dam. Cross dam and go up tarmac path past valve gear to gate.

❻ Go through gate on **R**, then through wall gap and up path. This runs alongside road to car park. Where path ends there's another up **L**, signed for Clough Head. Go up, meeting access road again, then continue up steps and through plantation just below main road. Go **L** up road for 50yds (46m) then cross it by footpath sign to kissing gate opposite. Short footpath leads back to start.

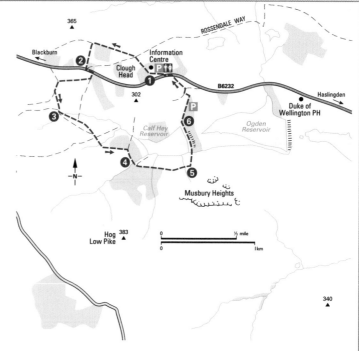

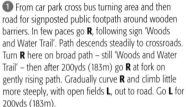

DARWEN TOWER Freedom Of The Moors

A simple walk, if moderately steep in parts, to a great landmark on the moors.

4 miles/6.4km 1hr 30min **Ascent** 705ft/215m **Difficulty** 2

Paths Well-defined tracks throughout, 1 stile
Map OS Explorer 287 West Pennine Moors **Grid ref** SD 665215
Parking Pay car park near Royal Arms

❶ From car park cross bus turning area and then road for signposted public footpath around wooden barriers. In few paces go **R**, following sign 'Woods and Water Trail'. Path descends steadily to crossroads. Turn **R** here on broad path – still 'Woods and Water Trail' – then after 200yds (183m) go **R** at fork on gently rising path. Gradually curve **R** and climb little more steeply, with open fields **L**, out to road. Go **L** for 200yds (183m).

❷ Go **R** up walled track on far side of Fine Peters Farm. Go straight on at junction then descend steeply, with section of old paving, towards Earnsdale Reservoir. Cross dam and swing **L** at its end then follow lane up **R** until it swings **L** once more, over cattle grid. Go straight up steep grass slope ahead, skirting fenced area with regenerating trees.

❸ Go **L** on track then, just above Water House, bear **R** to walk up concrete track. At gap in aluminium barrier bear **L** on level path to old quarry. Once there, go up **R** on stony track then, above sign, keep **L** where it forks. Gate on **L** gives good view of town of Darwen, dominated by India Mill chimney. Continue up main track for another 100yds (91m). As gradient eases and tower comes into view bear **R**, past marker stone bearing likeness of tower, and straight up to real thing.

❹ From tower bear **L** past trig point and then along broad path above steeper slope that falls to Sunnyhurst Hey Reservoir. Where path swings **L**, by 2nd bench, take 2nd path on **R**, overlooking valley of Stepback Brook and go down zig-zag path. Don't cross stile ahead but go back **L**, and finally over stile at bottom. Go **L** on track to cross stream.

❺ Track swings back **R** and up through wood. As it levels pass **R** of pair of gates and continue down towards houses. Lane just **L** of these leads to road. Go back past bus turning area to car park.

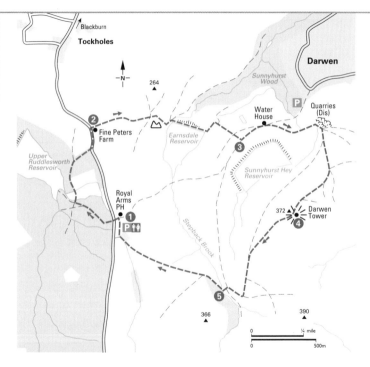

WYCOLLER Weaving Ways

Around a district steeped in the history of the textile industry.

5.25 miles/8.4km 2hrs **Ascent** 538ft/164m ⚠ **Difficulty** 2
Paths Field paths, some rough tracks and quiet lanes, 19 stiles
Map OS Explorer OL21 South Pennines **Grid ref** SD 926395
Parking Car park just above Wycoller village

1 At top of car park are noticeboard and sign 'Wycoller 500m'. Follow footpath indicated, just above road, until it joins it on bend. Cross 1st of 2 stiles on **R** and slant **R** across field to another stile, then up to gate and into garden. Follow arrow through trees up **L** side to another stile.

2 Bear **R**, past Bracken Hill house, then go **L** to cross stream, up towards house on skyline, until footbridge and stile appear in dip. Follow hedge and then wall in same line. When it ends at open, rushy pasture bear slightly **R** (towards Pendle Hill, if clear). Cresting rise, you'll see stile and signpost by corner of walls. Sign for Trawden points too far **R**. Aim slightly **L**, between 2 power line poles and again, once over rise, you'll see stile and signpost by end of fine wall. Follow wall and then walled track to Higher Stunstead. Go past 1st buildings and into yard.

3 Go **L** up walled track to cattle grid then keep ahead to stile and alongside stream up to Little Laith. Go past

house on **L** then go **R**, through 2nd gate, along field edges, to large barn on skyline by New Laith. Follow arrows round farm.

4 Continue straight ahead to stile by gate and over more stiles to Mean Moss. Go few paces **L** up track then follow wall on **R** and more stiles to Beaver. Go slightly **R** down field to stile near corner then up by stream to track.

5 Go **L**, then keep straight on by wall following rougher track (Pendle Way sign). When wall turns sharp **L**, track bends gradually, above stream.

6 At Access Land notice go slightly **L** to stile by gate then take lower path, down towards stream then up round wood. From kissing gate drop down to cross stream, then follow it down and out to lane.

7 Go **L** down lane to visitor centre and Wycoller. From here, continue along lane and join outward part of route for last 350yds (320m) to car park.

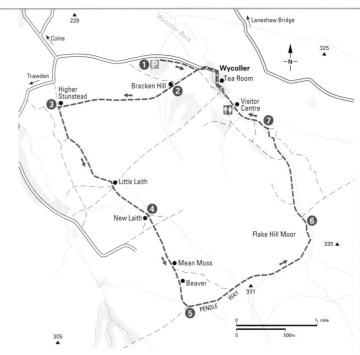

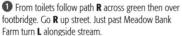

PENDLE HILL Witching Ways

A grand loop around the flanks and ridges of Pendle Hill.

4.75 miles/7.7km 2hrs **Ascent** 738ft/225m ⚠ **Difficulty** ③
Paths Field paths and rough moorland, surfaced track, 11 stiles
Map OS Explorer OL21 South Pennines; Explorer OL41 Forest of Bowland & Ribblesdale
Grid ref SD 823403 **Parking** Public pay car park in Barley village

❶ From toilets follow path **R** across green then over footbridge. Go **R** up street. Just past Meadow Bank Farm turn **L** alongside stream.

❷ Keep straight on up; cross footbridge and join lane. Go **L** and follow this well-signposted route past building then up to Brown House. Go into yard, **R** on track for 60yds (55m) then **L** through kissing gate. Follow obvious path through small hollow with newly planted trees and up to gate **L** of Pendle House.

❸ Go **L**; meet path just above wall. After next gate, climb, away from wall. Path undulates, then dips more definitely and meets wall again. From stile (don't cross it) above Under Pendle, bear **R** and follow fence. Cross stream then straight on up clearer track to rejoin wall.

❹ Bear **R** on trackway climbing alongside obvious groove. Beyond 2 old wooden gateposts, go **L** through 5-bar gate (not kissing gate) and straight downhill with wall on **L**. Cross track and descend steeply to gate just below Upper Ogden Reservoir.

❺ Follow reservoir road until just above Lower Ogden Reservoir. Go **R** over bridge, down steps then round **R** to footbridge. Climb steps and then go **L** to climb steps through plantation. At its end go up **R** to ridge.

❻ Turn **L** following fence then wall. Beyond wall gate veer **R**, keeping roughly level until rooftops of Newchurch appear. Aim for water trough, then stile and signpost. Descend short path to road.

❼ Go down road opposite (Jinny Lane). After 100yds (91m) cross stile on **L-H** side and follow rising footpath. Fork to **L** just inside plantation. At far end of plantation keep straight on, gradually converging with wall on **L-H** side. Follow wall, changing sides half-way along, to join sunken track. Cross this and descend to road.

❽ Go down tarmac track opposite, cross Pendle Water then go **L** alongside it. Continue on stonier track past cottages and converted mill. Finally short path on **R** leads back to car park.

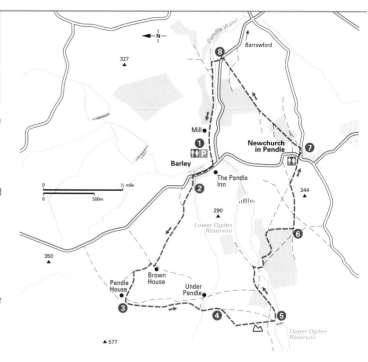

HODDER VALLEY The Forest Of Bowland
Around the heart of the Forest of Bowland.

7 miles/11.3km 2hrs 30min **Ascent** 853ft/260m ⚠ **Difficulty** [2]
Paths Field paths, farm tracks and quiet lane, 12 stiles
Map OS Explorer OL41 Forest of Bowland & Ribblesdale **Grid ref** SD 658468
Parking Roadside parking near Inn at Whitewell or below church

1 From lower parking area follow riverbank **L** to stepping stones. Climb just **R** of woods and through farmyard of New Laund. By old cheese press go **L** on curving track below slopes, then up field. Bear **L** to gate on to lane. Go few paces **L** to stile on **R**.

2 Cross rough pasture, aiming just **L** of house, then go **R** on surfaced track, swinging round into little valley. Go **L** to farm, then **R**, through farmyard to footbridge.

3 Turn **L**, past chicken coops, to stile on **R**. Cross field corner to another stile then go straight on to Dinkling Green Farm. A gap to **R** of cow shed leads into farmyard.

4 Half-way down yard go **R**, between buildings, to ford. Keep **L** past plantation, follow next **R-H** field edge then go through gate in dip. Follow hedge round then cross it via gate and over rise. Bear **R**, down to beck, then up lane to Lickhurst Farm.

5 Turn **L** into farmyard then bear **R** and straight on down track. When it swings **R**, go **L** before next gate then straight ahead on intermittent track.

6 Just before Knot Hill Quarry, turn **L**, past lime kiln, to junction. Go **R** and down to lane. Go **L** then **L** again, round bend and down. Cross bridge on **R** and head **R** towards Stakes farm, crossing river on stepping stones.

7 Turn **L** and climb above river. At next junction cross stile and turn **L**, descend steeply, then swing **R**, slightly above River Hodder, to stile. Beyond ford go up faint track and keep climbing past **R** edge of plantation. Keep straight on across open field to stile in furthest corner.

8 Turn **L** then go through iron gate on **R**. Bear **L** and contour round hill, just above fence, to gates. After 100yds (91m) go **L** down through aluminium gate. Track swings **R**. Just past Seed Hill Cottage turn **L** and descend steps by burial ground. Short steep lane descends to start.

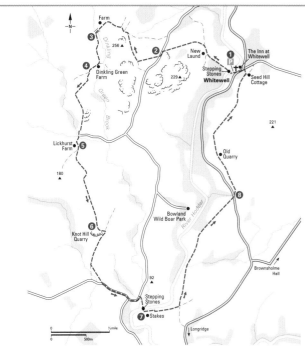

DUNSOP BRIDGE Moors At The Centre

This is a tough walk on the high moors.

9.25 miles/14.9km 3hrs 30min **Ascent** 1,247ft/380m **⚠ Difficulty** ③
Paths Field paths, rougher moorland paths, surfaced road, 10 stiles
Map OS Explorer OL41 Forest of Bowland & Ribblesdale **Grid ref** SD 662501
Parking Public car park at Dunsop Bridge

❶ From car park, go up surfaced track, passing just **L** of local post office and tea room, for about 800yds (732m). At end of track, by houses, follow public footpath ahead for another 100yds (91m) and then turn **R**, up steep bank.

❷ Cross field, bearing slightly **L** to meet power lines. Continue to stile before Beatrix farm. Follow track to just before 2nd set of buildings. Go **L**, through 2nd of 2 gates. Climb slope **R** of small stream, over stile, then follow wire fence across hillside. Drop into Oxenhurst Clough then climb out through plantation, rejoining fence as gradient eases. Keep straight on to join track.

❸ Go **L**; follow track to Burn House, where it swings **R**. Bear away **L**, slanting down and across open field, towards middle of young plantation. Follow path through it, bearing **R** to stile. Aim just **R** of another young plantation in dip, then cross field towards house (Laythams). Go **L** on lane for 300yds (274m).

❹ Turn **L** up metalled track. Clearly marked gates

guide you round Burnside Cottage. About 50yds (46m) above this, drop to stream and continue up to its **L**. From top of enclosure path rises to **R** alongside obvious groove, then swings back **L**. Climb steadily up ridge and then swing **R** above upper reaches of Dunsop Brook. Cross broad plateau, roughly parallel to old wall, to circular patch of stones.

❺ Turn **L**; cross wall at gate. Path beyond is clear. After slight rise it descends. As ground really steepens, descend in big zig-zags, with gate half-way down. Just above farm at Whitendale go **L** beside wall.

❻ Follow conspicuously level track for 0.75 mile (1.2km) until it swings round little side valley, over 2 footbridges. Cross stile and wind down to track by river. Follow this down to bridge by some waterworks.

❼ Cross bridge, join road and follow it steadily down valley for 1.5 miles (2.4km), past Bishop's House.

❽ After cattle grid, cross river on substantial footbridge. Just beyond this rejoin outward route.

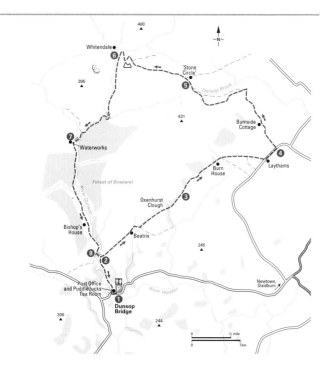

HURST GREEN Maybe Middle Earth

Did these rivers, fields and woods inspire Tolkien's creation of The Shire?

6.5 miles/10.4km 2hrs **Ascent** 459ft/140m ⚠ **Difficulty** ☐2
Paths Grassy riverside paths, woodland and farm tracks, 11 stiles
Map OS Explorer 287 West Pennine Moors **Grid ref** SD 684382
Parking By Hurst Green village hall or on roadside adjacent

❶ Walk down road to centre of Hurst Green. Cross main road and go down **L** of The Shireburn pub to stile below main car park. Go down edge of field and then follow small stream to reach duckboards and footbridge. After slight rise, descend via stile and winding path to River Ribble. Bear **L** just above river.

❷ Skirt aqueduct and return to riverbank. Join surfaced drive past Jumbles Rocks. Cross large wooden stile beyond small stone building to rejoin riverbank and follow it, towards Boat House.

❸ After rounding big bend, go up slightly to track. Follow this for 0.5 mile (800m). Opposite confluence of the Ribble and the Hodder, cross stile by bench.

❹ Narrow path quickly rejoins track. At Winkley Hall Farm go **L** to houses, **R** between barns then **L** past pond and out into lane. This climbs steeply then levels out, swinging **L** past Winkley Hall. Go through kissing gate on **R** and across field to another. Keep straight on across field, just **L** of wood, then down via stile and up to road.

❺ Turn **R** down pavement to river. Immediately before bridge, turn **L** along track. Follow river round, climb up past Hodder Place then descend again to bridge across stream.

❻ Go up track on **L**, cross footbridge and then climb wooden steps. Follow top edge of plantation then cross stile into field. Keep to its edge and at end cross stile into stony track. Keep **L**, past Woodfields and out to road. Go down track by post-box to Hall Barn Farm and along **R** side of buildings.

❼ Turn **R** and walk along tarmac track for 200yds (183m). Go **L** through gate by end of wall and along field. Drop down to **R** on track alongside wood then up to kissing gate. Follow field edge to kissing gate. At top of final field, through gate, narrow path leads to short lane. At its end turn **L** back to start of walk.

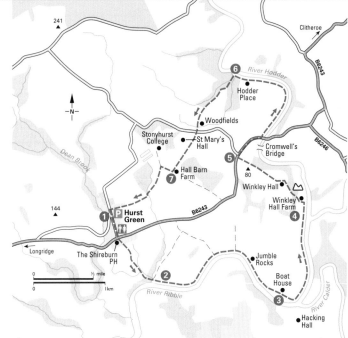

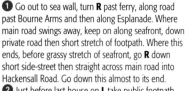

KNOTT END Breezy Brine Fields

An easy walk exploring an unexpected corner of Lancashire's coastal path.

5.5 miles/8.8km 1hr 45min **Ascent** 115ft/35m ⚠ **Difficulty** ☐1

Paths Quiet streets and lanes, farm tracks and sea wall, 3 stiles

Map OS Explorer 296 Lancaster, Morecambe & Fleetwood **Grid ref** SD 347485

Parking Free car park by end of B5270 at Knott End

❶ Go out to sea wall, turn **R** past ferry, along road past Bourne Arms and then along Esplanade. Where main road swings away, keep on along seafront, down private road then short stretch of footpath. Where this ends, before grassy stretch of seafront, go **R** down short side-street then straight across main road into Hackensall Road. Go down this almost to its end.

❷ Just before last house on **L** take public footpath which, beyond woodland, becomes straight track. Follow this through thin belt of trees, across fields and then beside wooded slope. Where wood ends go through iron kissing gate on **R** then up edge of wood and over stile into farmyard of Curwens Hill farm. Keep ahead through this and down stony track, which swings **L** between pools. It becomes surfaced lane past cottages.

❸ Join wider road (Back Lane) and go **R**. It becomes narrow again. Follow lane for about 1 mile (1.6km), over slight rise and down again, to Corcas Farm.

❹ Turn **R** on Corcas Lane, signed 'Private Road Bridle Path Only'. Follow it through brine fields. After 0.5 mile (800m) it swings **L** by caravan site.

❺ Go **R**, past Wyre Way sign and over stile on to embankment. Follow its winding course for about 1 mile (1.6km) to stile with signpost beyond.

❻ Keep ahead on clear tractor track under power lines. When it meets golf course, track first follows its **L** side then angles across – heed danger signs! Follow track to **R** of Hackensall Hall. Just past main gates go **L** on track with Wyre Way sign. This skirts round behind outlying buildings.

❼ Path swings to **R** and then crosses golf course again. Aim for green shelter on skyline then bear **R** along edge of course. Skirt round white cottages, then go **L** to sea wall. Turn **R** along it, to return to car park.

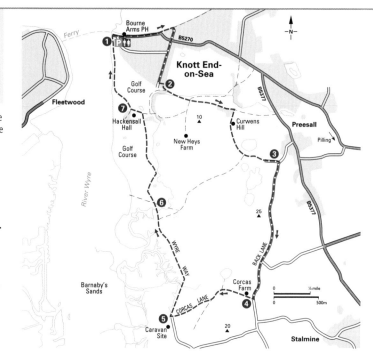

BEACON FELL The Bottom And The Top

Upland Lancashire countryside, by turns both expansive and intimate.

6 miles/9.7km 2hrs **Ascent** 689ft/210m ⚠ **Difficulty** ②
Paths Field paths, in places indistinct, clear tracks, 19 stiles
Map OS Explorer OL41 Forest of Bowland & Ribblesdale **Grid ref** SD 565426
Parking By Beacon Fell visitor centre

❶ Look for public footpath sign in **L-H** corner of lower car park by visitor centre. Go down broad, shady track, then through field. Bear **L** towards Crombleholme Fold and walk through farmyard. Turn **R** on to lane to bend.

❷ Go **L**, cross stream then up track swinging **R**. After 50yds (46m) go **L**, slanting gently down to stile just before field ends. Make for gate at far end of field then angle **R** to reach low bridge and up track beyond.

❸ Go through Cross Keys car park, through farmyard and into field. Go **R** to stile then straight on to corner of hedge. Follow it to tree then angle **L** to stile. Go **R** then straight ahead to lane and go **L**.

❹ Go **R** to Lower Trotter Hill. Cross cattle grid, go **L**, then round to **R** and past house. Go through **L-H** gate and up to stile. Follow field edge, eventually bending **L**. Go down stony track and then turn **R** on road.

❺ As road bends **R** keep walking straight ahead. Descend on sunken track through woods and cross footbridge. Go up few paces, then **R**, and follow obvious paths near river to reach Brock Mill picnic area.

❻ Cross bridge then go through gateway on **L**. Bear **R** up track then go **R**, through rhododendrons. Follow edge of wood, then go **R**, crossing stream. Go up field edge and straight on towards Lower Lickhurst. Go round into drive and up to road. Go **L** for few paces, then **R**, up drive. Keep straight on as it bends **L**, up fields to lane. Go **R** for 140yds (128m).

❼ Go **L** over stile and diagonally to isolated thorn tree. Continue almost level gateway and then to stile and footbridge. Follow old boundary, now muddy depression, then bear **L** to power lines. Follow these to marker post. Go **R**, directly uphill. Cross road to track rising through forest. At junction go **L** for 200m (183m) then **R** up narrow path to summit trig point.

❽ Bear **R** along forest edge then **L** across boardwalk. Keep ahead to return to visitor centre.

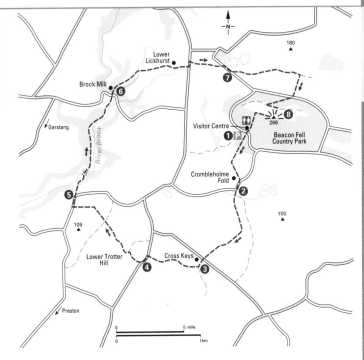

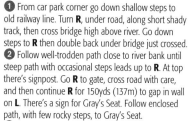

CROOK O'LUNE The Picturesque Crook O'Lune

A well-loved beauty spot.

3.25 miles/5.3km 1hr 15min **Ascent** 164ft/50m ⚠ **Difficulty** ☐1
Paths Tracks, pavement, woodland and field paths, 5 stiles
Map OS Explorer OL41 Forest of Bowland & Ribblesdale **Grid ref** SD 522647
Parking At Crook O'Lune, just off A683

❶ From car park corner go down shallow steps to old railway line. Turn **R**, under road, along short shady track, then cross bridge high above river. Go down steps to **R** then double back under bridge just crossed.
❷ Follow well-trodden path close to river bank until steep path with occasional steps leads up to **R**. At top there's signpost. Go **R** to gate, cross road with care, and then continue **R** for 150yds (137m) to gap in wall on **L**. There's a sign for Gray's Seat. Follow enclosed path, with few rocky steps, to Gray's Seat.
❸ Return down enclosed path to road, back along pavement, and cross again, back to signpost and through gate.
❹ Go **R**, level and almost parallel to road but soon descending, with steps, back towards river. Path levels and then forks. Swing **L** through fine grove of beech trees, and over small footbridge and stile to leave woods. Follow path along river bank. Cross small side stream, Escow Beck, by footbridge and follow curving

river bank past picnic tables. Go up to kissing gate, cross road; go through a gate almost opposite.
❺ Bear **L** down towards river, over footbridge, then round to **R** under old railway bridge. It's easy going now, following river bank upstream for over 0.75 mile (1.2km) to Artle Beck. This is crossed by arched footbridge.
❻ Continue up river bank for 440yds (402m) to waterworks bridge. Go round to stile at far side of small building, through kissing gate and up steps. Cross catwalk.
❼ At end of bridge drop down **L**. (A diversion into first wood is worth the effort, especially in bluebell season.) Follow river bank briefly then bear **R** to bridge. Keep on level across next field to stile at its far end. Go over this into another wood and follow clear path through it. All that remains is to follow river bank back to bridges and car park.

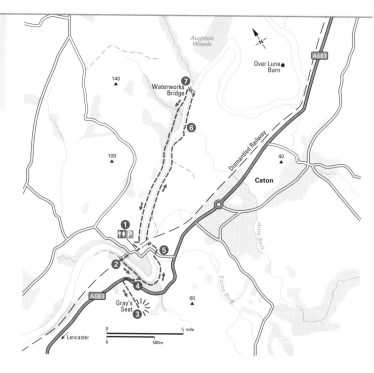

CLOUGHA PIKE Down To The Summit

A wild walk to an unrivalled landscape.

5.25 miles/8.4km 2hrs **Ascent** 1,050ft/320m ⚠ **Difficulty** ③

Paths Mostly very rough moorland, often rocky, 4 stiles

Map OS Explorer OL41 Forest of Bowland & Ribblesdale **Grid ref** SD 526604

Parking Access Area car park at Birk Bank

❶ Follow track above car park, then fork **L**. It becomes green path, running generally level, to Ottergear Bridge.

❷ Turn **L** and walk along level track, then bear **R** at next junction. Track climbs slightly, descends into valley, then climbs steeply up far side before it finally eases and swings round **R**.

❸ Go **L** on narrow path, running almost level above steeper slope. After 500yds (457m), it angles back down into valley. Follow base of steep slope and cross stream. After 30yds (27m) green track climbs to **R**.

❹ Wind up steeply to near-level moor. Path follows slight groove, then skirts **L** around boggy patch parallel to wall. Grassy path ahead is initially faint. Keep just **L** of continuous heather and it soon becomes clearer. There's another grooved section then clear stony path rises **L** across steeper ground.

❺ As slope eases path remains clear, passing few sketchy cairns. Follow groove, past tumbledown shooting butts. As ground levels, ease **R** past cairns

and marker stakes to ugly new track. Cross and follow thin grassy path with marker stakes. Bear **R** up slight rise and join wider path at cairn. Go **R** on broad ridge, crossing fence, to summit trig point.

❻ Descend clear path on **R** past large cairn. There's steep drop nearby on **L**, with small crags. Fence converges from **R**, eventually meeting wall.

❼ Scramble down rocks by end of wall. Continue down its **L** side for about 300yds (274m). Bear **L** at levelling amid scattered boulders. Descend through gap flanked by wrinkled rocks then across gentler slopes to gate by corner of wall.

❽ Head straight down until ground steepens, then swing **R** and weave down towards Windy Clough. From stile go **L** down grooved path to young trees. Fork **L**, closer to stream, rejoining wetter alternative routes above larger oaks. Descend through gorse then follow duckboards skirting bog. Turn **R** along track then **L** over slight rise to car park.

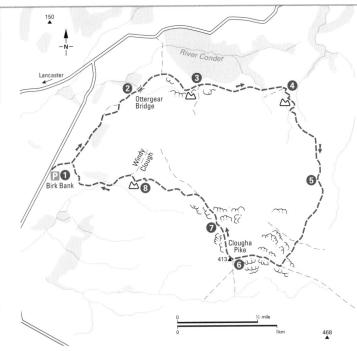

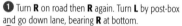

Lancashire • NORTHERN ENGLAND

LECK BECK Over The Underground
The subterranean mysteries of limestone.

7.5 miles/12.1km 3hrs **Ascent** 968ft/295m ⚠ **Difficulty** 3
Paths Field paths, indefinite moorland paths, quiet road, 5 stiles
Map OS Explorer OL2 Yorkshire Dales – Southern & Western **Grid ref** SD 643767
Parking Park by Leck church (honesty box)

❶ Turn **R** on road then **R** again. Turn **L** by post-box and go down lane, bearing **R** at bottom.

❷ At end of tarmac take lower, **L** track to stile then continue on good tractor track. Just after crossing stream track divides. Go **L** through gate into wood then through long pasture, passing wooden house. Cross stile at far end into 'open access' country. Track descends almost to river level then climbs away.

❸ Climb fairly steeply for 300yds (274m) then go **L** in slight dip past ruins of Anneside. Path, now little more than sheep track, runs fairly level and straight to meet ruined wall. Cross dip of small stream then bear **L** out of it, crossing damp ground on to grassy shoulder. Follow crest of steeper slopes dropping towards beck to arrive at brink of tree-filled gorge.

❹ Go straight ahead on narrow path across slope. It's not difficult, but it's clearly no place to slip. This leads into upper reaches of Ease Gill Kirk. Look around, then retrace to crossroads and descend to more level area

below small outcrops. Cross steep grass slope into gorge. After exploring return to crossroads.

❺ Now head directly southeast uphill (not track above gorge) taking sharp **R** on faintest of paths through bracken and heather to ruined wall. Follow this up to **L** then along, above rocky outcrops to green conical pit. Keep trending uphill and to **R**, on sheep tracks, to meet long, straight, dry-stone wall. Follow this until fenced holes appear in shallow dip on **L**. Bear **L** to nearest one, then follow narrow footpath past 2nd and 3rd. Follow shallow valley with no permanent stream to deep, fenced shaft (Rumbling Hole).

❻ Turn **R** on faint footpath across moorland to fenced hole, about 200yds (183m) away (Short Drop Cave). Now head back towards dry-stone wall and, just before it, head up **L** to join road. Turn **R** to walk down it. After 150yds (137m) Lost John's Cave is seen **L**.

❼ Continue down quiet road for 2.5 miles (4km) back to Leck. Turn **L** near church to return to start.

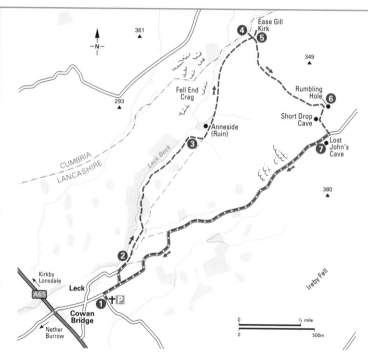

SILVERDALE A Quart In A Pint Pot

Enjoy continuous changes of scenery.

5.5 miles/8.8km 2hrs **Ascent** 426ft/130m ⚠ **Difficulty** ☒2
Paths Little bit of everything, 9 stiles
Map OS Explorer OL7 The English Lakes (SE) **Grid ref** SD 472759
Parking Small National Trust car park for Eaves Wood

❶ From end of car park, follow footpath to T-junction. Go **R** few paces and then turn **L**, climbing gently. Keep **L** to beech ring, then straight on. Just beyond junction veer **L** to wall and continue walking on this line to lane.

❷ Cross on to track signed 'Cove Road'. Keep ahead down path (Wallings Lane), drive, another track and then narrow path to wider road. After 200yds (183m) go **L** down Cove Road.

❸ From Cove walk **L**, below cliffs, to shore. Walk up road to Beach Garage then take footpath alongside. (If high tide makes route impassable follow easy footpath across fields above.)

❹ At next road turn **R** for 600yds (549m) then bear **R** down Gibraltar Lane for 350yds (320m). Enter National Trust property of Jack Scout.

❺ Descend **L** to lime kiln then follow narrowing path directly away from it. This swings **L** above steep drop and descends. Follow broad green path to gate. After 150yds (137m), another gate leads into lane. At end continue below Brown's Houses along edge of salt marsh to stile.

Go up slightly, then along to signpost.

❻ Turn **L**, climbing steeply to gate. Gradient eases, over rock and through lightly wooded area into open. Go **L** to stile then follow wall down and into small wood. Follow track down **R**. Cross road to wall gap, descend, then walk below crags to Woodwell.

❼ Path signed 'The Green via cliff path' leads to rocky staircase. At top go ahead to broader path. Follow it **L**, slant **R**, then continue into woodland. Stile on **R** and narrow section lead to road. Go **R** 150yds (137m), then **L** into The Green. Keep **R** at junction then join wider road.

❽ Go **L** for 75yds (69m) then **R**, signposted 'Burton Well Lambert's Meadow'. Track soon descends then swings **L**, passing Burton Well on **R**. Cross stile into Lambert's Meadow, then go **R**, over footbridge to gate. Climb up, with steps, and continue more easily to fork. Go **L** alongside pool (Bank Well) into lane. Go **L** and at end car park is almost opposite.

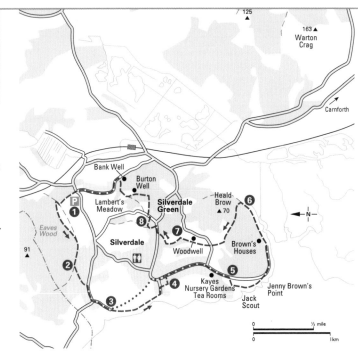

KENDAL Two Castles

Visit two ancient castles.

3 miles/4.8km 1hr 30min **Ascent** 300ft/91m ⚠ **Difficulty** 1
Paths Pavements, surfaced and grassy paths with steps, no stiles
Map OS Explorer OL7 The English Lakes (SE) **Grid ref** SD 518928 **Parking** Free parking area by river (occasionally occupied by fairground), numerous pay car parks near by

1 Walk upstream along riverside parking area to footbridge crossing river. Cross and bear **L** to follow surfaced walkway, through Gooseholme. At junction of roads beyond Church of St George turn **R** down Castle Street. Pass Castle Inn and Ann Street, keeping **R** and continuing up hill to Castle Road on **R**. Ascend Castle Road to where kissing gate on **R** leads on to Castle Hill. Follow broad path uphill to ruins of Kendal Castle.

2 Round castle ruins until, at point beneath its southern end, path is found dropping down to **R**. Descend steeply to pass through kissing gate on to Sunnyside. Go down road over old canal bridge and emerge on Aynam Road.

3 Turn **R** along Aynam Road to crossing. Cross and find footbridge leading over River Kent. Over river bear **L**, downstream, and walk past Abbot Hall to narrow, surfaced path leading **R**. Take this path, lined by yew trees and limestone coping stones, to pass between Kendal parish church and Abbot Hall

Art Gallery. Emerge on to Kirkland Road, main road through Kendal, by impressive gates of church with Ring O'Bells pub **L**. Turn **R** along road and proceed 150yds (137m) to crossing. Cross it then bear **R** to cross Gillingate and keep along main road, now called Highgate. At Lightfoot's chemist shop go **L** up Captain French Lane for 300yds (274m), then **R** up Garths Head. Follow this until steep path ascends **L**. Steps lead to terrace and view over Kendal. Cross grass terrace towards mound and its bodkin-shaped obelisk. Climb steps then spiral **L** until, as tpath levels, steps lead up to **R** to obelisk and top of Castle Howe.

4 Return to path and go **R**. Find gap on **L** and emerge on road at top of Beast Banks. Descend hill, which becomes Allhallows Lane, to traffic lights and pedestrian crossing opposite Town Hall. Cross road and go **L** and then immediately **R** down Lowther Street. Go **L** at bottom to zebra crossing beyond the Holy Trinity of St George, which leads to riverside.

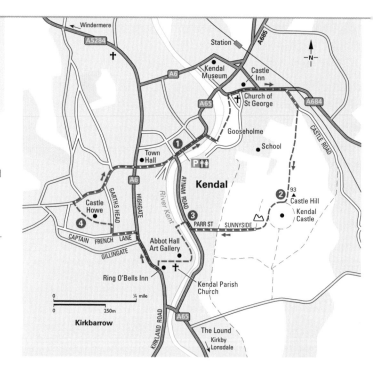

SEDGWICK The Lancaster Canal
Walking by the Lancaster Canal.

5.5 miles/8.8km 2hrs 30min **Ascent** 600ft/183m ⚠ **Difficulty** 1
Paths Field paths, towpaths and some quiet lanes, 10 stiles
Map OS Explorer OL7 The English Lakes (SE) **Grid ref** SD 513870
Parking Roadside parking in Sedgwick

1 From canal aqueduct, follow Natland Lane as far as 2nd junction by Carex Farm and turn **R**. At Crosscrake church, go **R** again, signed 'Stainton Cross'.

2 Leave through 1st gate on **L** and cross to stile in far **R** field corner. Follow **L-H** hedge, continuing upwards over 2nd stile. Beyond crest, drop to Skettlegill Farm, cross Stainton Beck and walk to lane beyond.

3 Cross to gate opposite between buildings and then pass through another gate ahead. Climb again to stile, and maintain direction across next field. Over another stile, walk to far wall and turn **R** to corner before emerging on to track by Summerlands.

4 Walk down track, passing through gate by Eskrigg Wood. Way shortly broadens into meadow, but keep going to further of 2 gates at **L** corner. Waymark confirms route along hedged track into rough woodland. Soon path bends **L** to stile near gate. Walk across field to track at far side.

5 Follow track to **R**, leading through small, gated farmyard at High Commonmire, and continuing beyond

as metalled way. Bear **R** at junction and carry on down to Field End Bridge.

6 Cross canal, drop **L** on to towpath and walk beneath bridge. Presently, beyond aqueduct, canal ends; onward section to Kendal has been filled in, de-watered or lost beneath road construction. However, its course remains clear, eventually leading to lane below A590.

7 Pass under bridge and rejoin canal through gate on **R**. Cutting leads to mouth of Hincaster Tunnel, where path **L** carries walkers, as it once did horses, over Tunnel Hill. At far side, turn **R** behind cottages to regain towpath. Remain by canal until forced on to lane and continue eventually to cross A590.

8 Just beyond bridge, steps rise to field on **R**. Walk ahead beside fence, and on across field, eventually passing beneath lone bridge. Beyond, canal cutting is again evident, accompanying you to Sedgwick, where steps beside aqueduct drop to road.

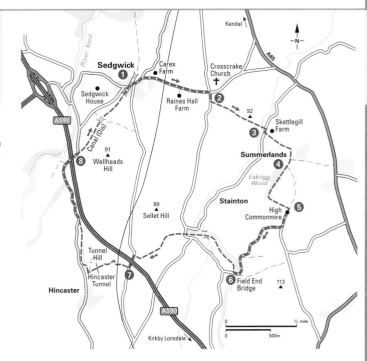

CUNSWICK SCAR Along The Limestone

The freedom of the heights, extensive views and varied flora, fauna and fossils make this an intriguing and liberating outing.

3 miles/4.8km 1hr 30min **Ascent** 250ft/79m ⚠ **Difficulty** ☐1

Paths Paths and tracks, can be muddy, take care as edge of scar is unguarded in places, 2 stiles
Map OS Explorer OL7 The English Lakes (SE) **Grid ref** SD 489923
Parking Beneath radio mast near top of hill

❶ Walk away from road, cross sloping limestone bed that forms car park and take track that leads to communications mast. Pass low barrier then bear **R** to follow narrow path through wood. Leave wood by kissing gate at junction of stone walls. Look for footpath sign 'Cunswick Fell'. Enter field and continue by stone wall. At corner of field go **R** and follow path parallel to wall. Continue over humpback of field and drop to pass gate, beyond which wall turns sharp corner.

❷ Continue ahead on grassy path for 30yds (27m) then follow it round **L**, aiming for lone fingerpost. Ignore **R** turn and stay with track over brow and down to gate in fence. Go through gate and follow wall on **R** as it descends to dip and round **R**. Beyond dip, path traces off **L** to join more prominent track. Turn **L** on

this and follow it to hilltop where you'll find summit cairn of Cunswick Scar, commanding viewpoint.

❸ Walk on beyond cairn and drop to lower terrace edged by scar. Take care here, cliff face of scar is unfenced here and reaches vertical height of around 40ft (12m). Turn **L**, facing out, and bear south along edge of scar. A fence now runs along crag edge. Keep along rim of scar through avenue of gorse and hazel to wall edge. Take narrow path alongside wall to stile crossing fence.

❹ Cross stile and continue by wall before bearing **L** to merge with original footpath at end of raised shoulder. Retrace steps to join dry-stone wall at its corner, with gate just beyond. Pass gate and follow path along by walls to kissing gate at edge of wood. Follow path **L** through wood.

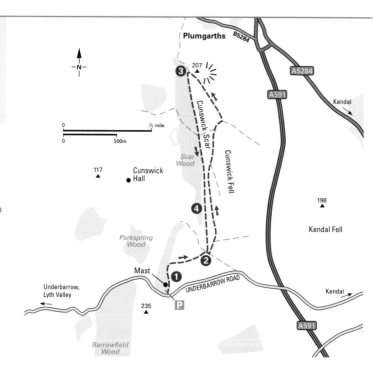

KENTMERE A Remote Valley

Once ravaged by Scottish reivers, this lovely remote valley now basks in tranquillity.

6.75 miles/10.9km 2hrs 15min **Ascent** 689ft/210m ⚠ **Difficulty** 2

Paths Generally good tracks and paths, some open fields, 7 stiles
Map OS Explorer OL7 The English Lakes (SE) **Grid ref** SD 456040
Parking Very limited in Kentmere, but small field by Low Bridge is occasionally available

❶ Begin on bridleway, marked 'Kentmere Hall', opposite St Cuthbert's Church. Approach farmyard, bear **R** behind cattle pens, then **R** through side gate. Signpost, 'Garburn and Reservoir', directs you up field. Leave at top and walk to gate. Pass barn and go through gap to gate, where track leads past Nook House.

❷ Ignore turn-off to Garburn, and immediately after next house (Greenhead) go **L**. Still following signs to reservoir, bear **R** through gate, and then **R** again at 2nd fork to join metalled track leading up valley.

❸ Valley bottom is wide and flat. Bear **L** past entrance to Hartrigg Farm and continue on track through valley, now progressively squeezed between craggy breasts of Yoke and Kentmere Pike. Eventually dam appears, rising above heaps of abandoned slate quarries.

❹ Continue to dam. Fed by waters from two boulder-strewn combes that divide the valley head, the reservoir is a wild and deserted place.

❺ Bridges below dam take return route across outflows to path just above, which then follows windings of Kent downstream. Beyond quarries, cross ladder stile into enclosure. Leave by gate on **L** by barn.

❻ Track continues through successive fields, eventually leading to Overend Farm. Ignore tarmac lane and bear **R** through gate on to grass track. Where track later drops from Hallow Bank, keep ahead along Low Lane.

❼ This delightful old track, its walls luxuriant with mosses and ferns, ultimately emerges on to lane. Carry on, at next junction, to waymarked stile on **R** little further along. Route now lies across field but, for snack, continue along lane to 2nd junction and turn **L** to Maggs Howe, above lane on **R**.

❽ Retrace your steps to stile and walk down to far bottom corner of field. Steep path drops beside stream through larch to emerge on to lane. Turn **L** and, at end, go **R**, to return to church.

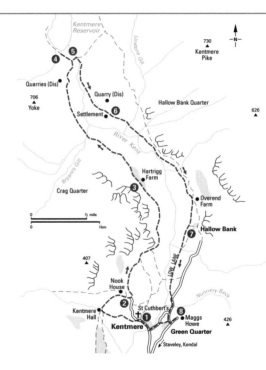

GRANGE-OVER-SANDS Above Hampsfell

A walk above a charming seaside resort.

4 miles/6.4km 2hrs **Ascent** 790ft/241m ⚠ **Difficulty** 2
Paths Paths and tracks, can be muddy in places, 7 stiles **Map** OS Explorer OL7 The English Lakes (SE)
Grid ref SD 410780 **Parking** Car park below road and tourist office in central Grange

❶ Join main road through Grange and go **R** (north), to pass gardens. Cross road and continue along pavement to roundabout. Go **L** along Windermere Road rising to round bend, and find steps up to squeeze stile on **L**, signed 'Routon Well/Hampsfield'.
❷ Take path through Eggerslack Wood. Cross over surfaced track and continue to pass house on **L**. Steps lead on to track. Cross this diagonally to follow track, signed 'Hampsfell'. Track zig-zags to **R** (with house **L**) and continues up through woods to stile over wall.
❸ Cross stile to leave wood and follow path up hillside. Pass limestone pavement sections and craggy outcrops until path levels and bears **L** to stile over wall. Cross stile and go **R** along wall. Continue, following track, to pass cairns and up to Hospice of Hampsfell.
❹ Leave tower, head south and follow path over edge of limestone escarpment (take care). Continue over another escarpment and descend to wall stile. Descend into dip; rise directly up green hill beyond.

Cross top and descend to wall stile. Path bears diagonally **L** here but it is usual to continue to cairn marking Fell End. Turn sharp **L** and descend to grassy track **L** round valley of thorn bushes to gate to road.
❺ Cross road, take squeeze stile and descend diagonally **L** across field to gate to road by front door of Springbank Cottage. Descend track to enter farmyard; continue **L** over stone stile. Go over hill, following path parallel to wall; take stile into ginnel. Follow this down, with high garden wall **R**, round corner; drop to road junction. Go **L** on private road/ public footpath; bear **R** at fork. At junction turn **R** to descend track; at next junction go **L** down Charney Well Lane. At next junction, turn **L** below woods of Eden Mount to junction with Hampsfell Road near hill bottom; turn **R**. At junction with larger road go **L** (toilets to **R**); pass church before descending to pass clock tower and junction with main road (B5277). Go **L** and then **R** to car park.

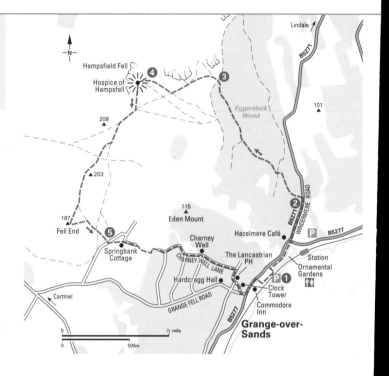

POOLEY BRIDGE A Roman Road

Enjoy views over the lake, cross a Roman road and spot the prehistoric artefacts.

4.5 miles/7.2km 2hrs **Ascent** 740ft/225m ⚠ **Difficulty** 2
Paths Surfaced roads, stony tracks, grassy tracks and hillside
Map OS Explorer OL5 The English Lakes (NE) **Grid ref** NY 470244
Parking Pay car parks either side of bridge

1 From bridge crossing River Eamont follow main street (B5320) through centre of Pooley Bridge. Walk on past church then turn **R** to follow pavement along Howtown Road.

2 At junction continue over crossroads. Road rises and becomes pleasantly tree-lined before ending at unsurfaced track beneath Roehead. Pair of gates lead on to open moor.

3 Go through 1 of gates and climb wide track, continuing to where going levels and track crosses High Street Roman road.

4 Bear **R** along resurfaced stretch of Roman road to reach low circular ancient wall of earth and stone. This, Cockpit, is largest of prehistoric antiquities on Moor Divock.

5 Way leads back diagonally north by shallow shake holes (sinkholes) to original track at Ketley Gate. (Little to **R**, White Raise burial cairn is worthy of attention.) Either follow track (route marked on map), which

leads off northeast ascending to walled wood high on hillside and then bear **L** to top of Heughscar Hill, or go **L** up well-worn path through bracken, starting by stone parish boundary marker. Flat hill summit occupies commanding position offering rewarding views.

6 Proceed north along high shoulder to pass broken little limestone crag of Heugh Scar below **L**. At end of scar make steep descent of grassy hillside crossing track and continuing down to point where another track and lane of High Street Roman road cross each other. Descend to **L** taking track which passes below Roman road and head in general direction of Ullswater. Note lime kiln and little quarry **L**. Continue descent to corner of wall marked by large sycamore tree. Follow route which falls steeply down beside wall. Bear **L** near bottom of incline and gain original broad track just above gates near Roehead. Return by same road back to Pooley Bridge.

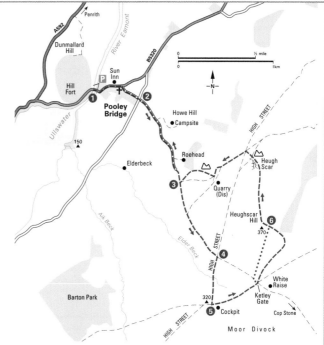

PATTERDALE Ullswater Shore

From the shore of Ullswater to one of its most spectacular viewpoints.

4 miles/6.4km 1hr 30min **Ascent** 490ft/150m ▲ **Difficulty** ☒2
Paths Stony tracks and paths, no stiles **Map** OS Explorer OL5 The English Lakes (NE)
Grid ref NY 396159 **Parking** Pay-and-display car park opposite Patterdale Hotel

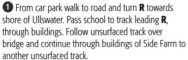

❶ From car park walk to road and turn **R** towards shore of Ullswater. Pass school to track leading **R**, through buildings. Follow unsurfaced track over bridge and continue through buildings of Side Farm to another unsurfaced track.

❷ Turn **L** along undulating track, with stone wall **L**, and pass through mixed woodland, predominantly oak and ash, before open fellside appears above. Proceed along path above campsite and pass stand of larch before descending to cross stream above buildings of Blowick, seen through trees below. Path ascends to crest craggy knoll above woods of Devil's Chimney. Make steep descent following path through rocks before it levels to traverse beneath craggy heights of Silver Crag. Slight ascent, passing fine holly trees, gains shoulder of Silver Point and outstanding view of Ullswater. Short there-and-back to tip is worthwhile.

❸ Follow path, which sweeps beneath end of Silver Crag and continue to pass small stream before steep stony path, eroded in places, breaks off to **R**. Ascend

this, climbing diagonally **R**, through juniper bushes. Gain narrow gap which separates Silver Crag to **R** from main hillside of Birk Fell to **L**. This valley is quite boggy and holds small tarnlet.

❹ To avoid steep, exposed ground, follow high narrow path to make gradual descent south in direction of Patterdale. But if you have head for heights, short steep scramble leads to top of Silver Crag. Care must be exercised for steep ground lies in all directions. Descend back to ravine and main path by same route. Path is easy though it traverses open fellside and may be boggy in places. Pass open quarry workings (large unfenced hole beside path: take care), and continue on to cross slate scree of larger quarry. Bear **R** to descend by stream and cross little footbridge leading to gate at end of track.

❺ Go **L** through gate and follow lane through meadows. Cross bridge and join road. Bear **R** through Patterdale to return to car park.

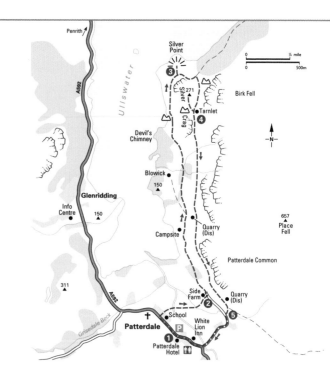

BOWNESS-ON-WINDERMERE Brant Fell

Enjoy woodlands and breathtaking views.

3.5 miles/5.7km 1hr 15min **Ascent** 525ft/160m ⚠ **Difficulty** 2
Paths Pavement, road, stony tracks, grassy paths, 2 stiles
Map OS Explorer OL7 The English Lakes (SE) **Grid ref** SD 398966
Parking Fee car park on Glebe Road above Windermere lake

❶ Take Glebe Road into Bowness town. Swing **L** and, opposite steamer pier, go **R** over main Windermere road; turn **L**. Opposite Church of St Martin turn **R** to go up St Martins Hill. Cross Kendal road to climb Brantfell Road directly above. At head of road iron gate leads on to Dales Way, which climbs directly up hillside. Continue to kissing gate by wood, leading on to lane.
❷ Pass through kissing gate and turn **R** ('Post Knott') to follow stony lane. Continue ahead rising through woods until lane crests height near flat circular top of Post Knott. Bear **L**; make short ascent to summit. Retrace steps to track; bear **R** to kissing gate, leaving wood on to open hillside.
❸ Beyond kissing gate take grassy path, rising to rocky shoulder. Cross shoulder and first descend, then ascend to ladder stile in top corner of field by fir trees. Cross stile then bear **R** to ascend up open grassy flanks of Brant Fell to rocky summit.

❹ Go **L** (northeast) from top of fell, following cairns to kissing gate. Descend through young plantation to 2nd gate and track. Turn **R** and follow track to stile and gate leading to road. Turn **L** along road and continue **L** at junction, to pass Matson Ground. Immediately beyond is kissing gate on **L**, waymarked for Dales Way.
❺ Go through kissing gate and continue down path to cross track and pass through kissing gate into next field. Keep along track beneath trees and beside new pond, until path swings **L** to emerge through kissing gate on to drive. Go **R** along drive for 30yds (27m) until path veers off **L** through trees to follow fence. Gate leads into field. Follow path, first descending and then rising to iron gate in field corner. Continue to join grassy track and go through kissing gate. Cross drive of Brantfell Farm and keep straight on to kissing gate leading into field. Follow path, parallel to wall, descending hill to intercept track, via kissing gate, and regain Point ❷. Retrace steps back to Glebe Road.

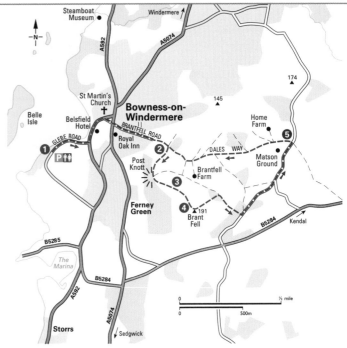

AMBLESIDE Lilies And Lakes

Above little Ambleside.

3.25 miles/5.2km 1hr 45min **Ascent** 575ft/175m ⚠ **Difficulty** ☐2

Paths Road, paths and tracks, can be muddy in places, 3 stiles

Map OS Explorer OL7 The English Lakes (SE) **Grid ref** NY 375047

Parking Ambleside central car park

❶ Take wooden footbridge from car park and go **R** along Rydal road past waterwheel and Bridge House. At junction bear **R** along Compston Road. Continue to next junction, with cinema on corner, then bear **R** to cross side road and enter Vicarage Road alongside chip shop. Pass school and enter Rothay Park. Follow main path through park to emerge by flat bridge over Stock Ghyll Beck. Cross this then go **L** to cross stone arched Miller Bridge spanning River Rothay.

❷ Bear **R** along road over cattle grid until, in few paces, steep surfaced road rises **L**. Climb road, which becomes unsurfaced, by buildings of Brow Head Farm. At S-bend beyond buildings, stone stile leads up and **L**. Pass through trees to find, in few dozen paces, stone squeeze stile. Pass through, cross little bridge and climb open hillside above. Paths are well worn and several routes are possible. For best views keep diagonally **L**. Rising steeply at first, path levels before rising again to ascend 1st rocky knoll. Cross stile and

higher, larger knoll offers good views.

❸ Beyond this, way descends to **R**, dropping to well-defined path. Followpath to pass little pond before cresting rise and falling to little Lily Tarn. Path skirts **R** edge of tarn, roughly following crest of Loughrigg Fell before joining wall on **L**. Follow this down through kissing gate and base of further knoll. This is ascended to another viewpoint.

❹ Take path descending **R** to prominent track below. Bear **R** to gate which leads through stone wall boundary of open fell and into field. Continue to descend track, passing old golf clubhouse. Intercept original route just above buildings of Brow Head.

❺ Continue to cross Miller Bridge then, before flat bridge, bear **L** to follow track alongside Stock Ghyll Beck. Beyond meadows lane through houses leads to main Rydal road. Bear **R** on road to car park beyond fire station.

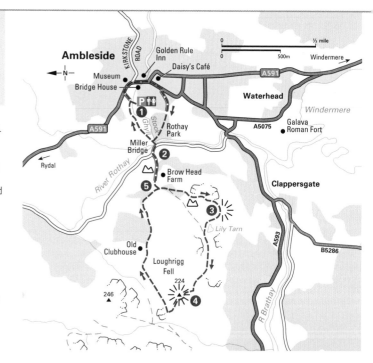

SOUTHER FELL A Bonnie Trail
Rolling grassy fells offer quiet solitude.

6 miles/9.7km 3hrs **Ascent** 985ft/300m ⚠ **Difficulty** 3
Paths Grassy and stony paths, open fellside, 4 stiles
Map OS Explorer OL5 The English Lakes (NE) **Grid ref** NY 364300
Parking Wide verge above river in Mungrisdale

❶ Head north on road, following Glenderamackin upstream. Bear **R** where road crosses bridge and continue to hairpin bend. Go **L** to leave road, pass telephone box; follow lane between cottages. Go through gate and along unsurfaced track above north. Now bear **L** and cross little Bullfell Beck by footbridge.
❷ Bear **L** off steeply ascending track and follow lesser stony track which traces route along **R** bank (true **L**) of Glenderamackin. Continue along track (boggy in places) to ford Bannerdale Beck. Easy to keep dry by balancing on stones. Round shoulder of Bannerdale Fell (White Horse Bent). Continue ascent until path falls **L** to flat wooden footbridge to cross River Glenderamackin.
❸ Path ascends hillside striking diagonally **L** to top of high grassy shoulder. Mousthwaite Comb lies below **R**. Bear **L**, following path and ascend long shoulder of Souther Fell. Pass large circular and continue along

level shoulder, heading north to summit (little rocky knoll).
❹ Keep north and continue to descend grassy nose of fell. Easy at first, angle steepens progressively until nearing base. Little craggy outcrops are best avoided by following path to their **L**. Path is well defined and soon leads to wall near fell bottom. Go **R** along by wall (path is extremely boggy in places). Continue along wall until it bends **L** and steep descent leads to surfaced road.
❺ Go **L** down road, through gate until, at hill bottom, grassy lane continues down to Glenderamackin, just upstream of buildings of Beckside. Before reaching ford that crosses river, stone steps over wall on **R** give access to narrow footbridge. Cross bridge, and then go **L** to exit field via squeeze stile. Go **R**, climbing grassy bank to road. Head **L** and upstream to return to parking area.

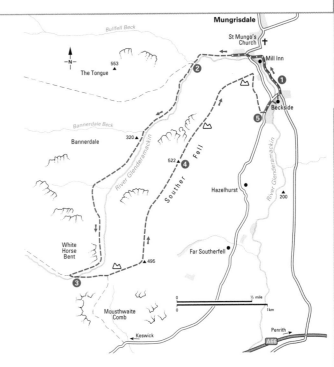

ST JOHN'S IN THE VALE A Wild Fell
Exploring a compact valley.

5 miles/8km 2hrs 45min **Ascent** 1,115ft/340m ▲ **Difficulty** 2
Paths Grassy paths and track, 8 stiles
Map OS Explorer OL5 The English Lakes (NE) **Grid ref** NY 318195
Parking Car park at Legburthwaite, head of St John's in the Vale

❶ Pass through head of car park to small gate leading on to old road. Turn **L**; go down lane to gate that opens on to verge of busy A591. Turn **R** and cross Smithwaite Bridge to stile climbing the wall to **R**. Cross stile and take path rising to **L**. This leads through stand of Scots pine and climbs to top of Wren Crag with fine views.

❷ Descend steeply into dip and take wall gap. Climb again to follow above rocky outcrops of Long Band. Grassy incline leads to stile over wire fence to **L**. Cross then follow it **R**, to pass tarn in hollow. Now descend to **L**, dipping to reach stile by wall junction. Beyond stile path runs along wall, climbing through corridor formed by rocky knoll of Moss Crag. Beyond crag boggy area forces you **L**. As you round it, turn **L** up steep slope to summit of High Rigg. Grassy ridge leads above tarns of Paper Moss to hollow and pond. Ascend to summit of Naddle Fell (unnamed on

Ordnance Survey maps), highest point of walk which offers a superb of high fells.

❸ Wide path falls down steepening hillside to buildings by road above St John's Church. Turn **R** down road past church to gate and stile leading to grassy track. Skirt foot of fell along track. Below Rake How pass a ruined farm.

❹ Keep along track taking high route **R** of and above Sosgill, to pass through 3 gates/stiles followed by kissing gate into plantation. Exit trees via kissing gate and continue to take path to **R** of Low Bridge End Farm. Continue along track through gates and stiles to where track meets bank of St John's Beck, beneath Wren Crag. Here track ends and footpath continues above river, rising through trees to grassy shoulder above stile that leads back on to A591. Turn **L** and **L** again to return to car park.

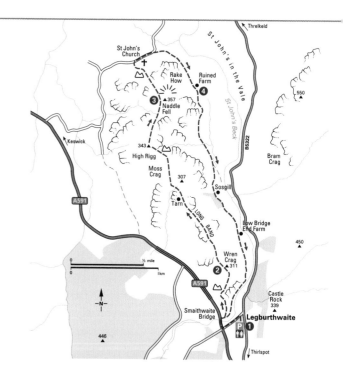

CONISTON To Tarn Hows

Explore Yewdale before reaching Tarn Hows.

6.75 miles/10.9km 3hrs 30min **Ascent** 885ft/270m ⚠ **Difficulty** 2
Paths Road, grassy paths and tracks, 4 stiles
Map OS Explorer OL7 The English Lakes (SE) **Grid ref** SD 303975
Parking Coniston car park by tourist information centre

❶ Exit the car park on to Tilberthwaite Avenue and turn **R**. Continue until road leads off to **L**. Follow this beyond football field to Shepherd Bridge. Cross; go immediately **L** over stone stile. Path leads to kissing gate into field. Bear diagonally **R** towards rocky outcrop oaks; continue along to **R** of wall. Shortly path leads to stone building.

❷ Pass building on **L**. Ascend through gate. Fork **R** following wall then rise to gate through (High Guards Wood perimeter). Climb steeply to top of. Cross ruined wall; follow waymarked path to descent through Guards Wood. Exit wood; continue on track, muddy in places, to gate and stile to stony lane.

❸ Go **L** up lane. Shortly, go **R** through gate. Rise with grassy track until it swings **R** through gate/stile. Vague grassy track intercepts fence with the larch plantation of Tarn Hows Wood below. Keep **R** along track; continue to steep, surfaced track. Tarn Hows Cottage is below to **L**. Go **R** to Tarn Hows road. Go **L**, ascending road past car park, to track bearing **L** above Tarn Hows.

❹ Follow track in anticlockwise circumnavigation of tarn. At end is little dam.

❺ Turn **R** here and descend path to **R** of beck. At bottom go **L** across footbridge then through Tom Gill car park to gate. Follow field-edge path to gate opposite Yew Tree Farm. Cross road and go **R** of farm, to gate. Rise to pass through another gate, then go **L** above fence. Keep along track, around High Yewdale Farm, until final gate on to Hodge Close road. Turn **L** over Shepherd's Bridge and join main Coniston road.

❻ Cross and go **L** until, opposite High Yewdale Farm, path leads **R** passing yew trees. Go **R** across fields. At Low Yewdale farmyard go **L** along lane, over bridge, and round sharp bend. Go **R** ('Cumbria Way'), through field. Beyond wall track ascends then bears **R**. Enter Back Guards Plantation and follow track through wood. Pass through yew trees. Descend to join outward route.

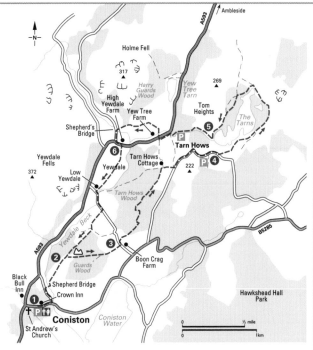

Cumbria • NORTHERN ENGLAND

SATTERTHWAITE Medieval Industry

Follow paths once trodden by charcoal burners, iron smelters and coppicers.

4.75 miles/7.7km 2hrs **Ascent** 1,017ft/310m ⚠ **Difficulty** 1
Paths Mainly good paths and tracks throughout, 3 stiles
Map OS Explorer OL7 The English Lakes (SE) **Grid ref** SD 344912
Parking Forest car park at Blind Lane

❶ Path from back of car park, marked by green- and white-topped posts, heads **R**, over rise to forest trail. Walk **L** and, after 400yds (366m), turn **L** on to path through birch wood. Go ahead over a junction at top and descend to metalled track into Satterthwaite.
❷ Turn **L** by church; walk through the village. After 0.25 mile (400m), at **L-H** bend, go **R** on to track, Moor Lane, and then at marker post, head **L** on to rising path into trees. Bear **L** at post and shortly drop to broader track.
❸ Go **R** over another hill and **R** again when you eventually reach broad forest trail. Pass waterfall. Beyond, track bends across stream before rising to junction. Turn **L** for 220yds (201m) and branch **L** again on to unmarked, descending grass track.
❹ Emerging on to lane at bottom, go **R**, then turn in between cottages at Force Forge. Through gate on **R**, go **L** by tall beech hedge and across Force Beck.

Continue through deer fence along winding path into Brewer Wood, bearing **R** at crossing path.
❺ After about 0.25 mile (400m), at fork, bear **L** to wall gap and carry on through trees. At indistinct fork beyond crest of hill take **R-H** branch, which descends to Rusland Reading Rooms. Cross to lane in front of church and walk **L**.
❻ After little way, leave lane for byway opposite junction. Climb over t top of Stricely beside wooded pastures and eventually drop to lane at Force Mills. Go **R** and then **L** to ascend beside Force Falls.
❼ At green and white post, part-way up hill, turn **R** on to path climbing steeply into larch plantation. Keep **R** where path forks, shortly passing through wall gap. Go through another gap few paces on and descend through trees back to car park.

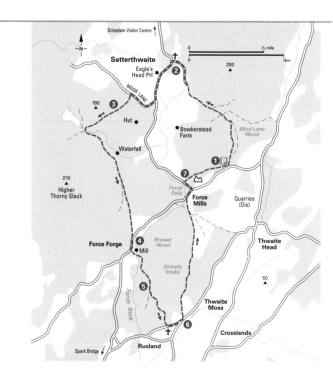

ELTER WATER Four Seasons Walk

Bluebell woods, a lake and Little Loughrigg.

4 miles/6.4km 2hrs **Ascent** 328ft/100m ⚠ **Difficulty** 2
Paths Grassy and stony paths and tracks, surfaced lane, 4 stiles
Map OS Explorer OL7 The English Lakes (SE) **Grid ref** NY 328048
Parking National Trust pay-and-display car park at Elterwater village

❶ Pass through small gate to walk downsteam above Great Langdale Beck. Continue to enter mixed woods of Rob Rash. Gate leads through wall (open foot of Elter Water lies **R**). Continue through the meadows above river. (Lane can be wet and is prone to flooding). Pass through gate and enter mixed woods. Keep along path to pass Skelwith Force waterfall down **R**. Little bridge leads across channel to viewing point above falls. Keep along path through industrial buildings (Kirkstone Quarry).

❷ Touchstone Gallery is on **R**, as path becomes surfaced road. Continue to intercept A593 by bridge over the river. Turn **L** to pass hotel. At road junction, cross Great Langdale road to lane that passes by end of cottages. Follow lane, ascending to intercept another road. Turn **R** (short distance) then **L** towards Tarn Foot farm. Bear **R** along track, in front of cottages. Where track splits, bear **L**. Through gate continue on track to

overlook Loughrigg Tarn. Half way along tarn cross stile over iron railings on **L**.

❸ Follow footpath down meadow to traverse **R**, just above tarn. Footpath swings off **R** to climb ladder stile over wall. Follow grassy track leading **R**, uphill, to gate and stile on to road. Turn **L** along road, until surfaced drive leads up to **R**, signed 'Public Footpath Skelwith Bridge'. Pass cottage and keep on track to pass higher cottage, Crag Head. Little way above, narrow grassy footpath leads **R**, up hillside, to gain level shoulder between craggy outcrops of Little Loughrigg.

❹ Cross shoulder and descend path, passing tarnlet to **R**, to intercept stone wall. Keep **L** along wall descending to find, in few hundred paces, ladder stile over wall into upper woods of Rob Rash. Steep descent leads to road. Cross this directly, and go through wall gap next to large double gates. Descend track to meet outward route. Bear **R** to return to Elterwater village.

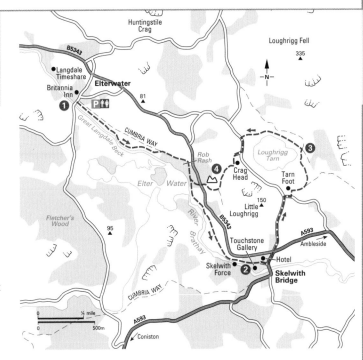

STONETHWAITE Herries Family Saga

Through Walpole's Herries Country – from Stonethwaite to Rosthwaite.

7.5 miles/12.1km 3hrs 30min **Ascent** 1,102ft/336m ⚠ **Difficulty** 2

Paths Bridleways, fairly good paths and some rough walking
Map OS Explorer OL4 The English Lakes (NW) **Grid ref** NY 262137
Parking By telephone box in Stonethwaite

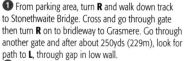

❶ From parking area, turn **R** and walk down track to Stonethwaite Bridge. Cross and go through gate then turn **R** on to bridleway to Grasmere. Go through another gate and after about 250yds (229m), look for path to **L**, through gap in low wall.

❷ Follow path up through wood, then cross stile and continue uphill on well-paved path through trees. Path emerges from trees still climbing. Cross stile beside Willygrass Gill and follow path to Dock Tarn.

❸ Ignore track going **R**, over beck, and continue on obvious path around **L** side of tarn. There are rocky sections but going isn't difficult. If lower path is flooded, higher paths to **L** lead in same direction.

❹ At north end of tarn broad path continues above boggy ground in direction of gap between 2 low crags. View opens up ahead with Ether Knott then Skiddaw beyond. Just past small rock pinnacle on **L**, Watendlath comes into view and path descends steep rocky staircase to kissing gate.

❺ Go through gate, cross beck and follow green-topped wooden posts on stone path across bog. Turn **R** at junction signed 'Watendlath' and descend to sheep pen. Go through wall gap and descend to kissing gate.

❻ Go through gate, follow stream downhill, cross then follow wall round field before turning **L** on to farm track. Go through 3 gates and turn **R** across old pack bridge into Watendlath.

❼ From Watendlath re-cross bridge and follow bridleway sign to Rosthwaite. Walk uphill on this well-used route, through kissing gate and head downhill, passing gate on **R** and going through another gate, lower down. At bottom of hill sign indicates that path continues to Stonethwaite.

❽ Ignore sign and instead turn **R** through gate in wall, go downhill, pass through another gate beside Hazel Bank Hotel then turn **L** on to public bridleway and follow this back to Stonethwaite Bridge.

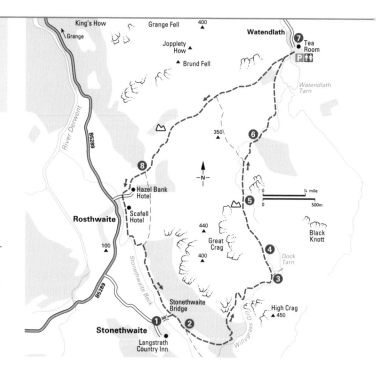

LATRIGG Taking The Line

A walk along a disused railway line leads to a fine viewpoint above Keswick.

5 miles/8km 2hrs **Ascent** 902ft/275m ⚠ **Difficulty** ▮1▮
Paths Railway trackbed, country lane, grassy fell paths, 3 stiles
Map OS Explorer OL4 The English Lakes (NW) **Grid ref** NY 270238
Parking At former Keswick Station

❶ From old Keswick Station, head along trackbed, away from Keswick. Beyond A66, here cantilevered above trackbed, route covers boardwalk section high above River Greta, before continuing to site of bobbin mill at Low Briery, now caravan site.

❷ Beyond Low Briery, River Greta is an agreeable companion as far as old railway building on **R** used as information point (with river bridge beyond). Before reaching building, turn **L** through gate and cross pasture to back lane. Turn **L** and climb, steeply for short while, to footpath signed 'Skiddaw', at gate and stile.

❸ Cross on to broad track swinging **R** round gorse bushes, and then running centrally up eastern ridge of Latrigg. Look back here for spectacular views. Short way on reach plantation on **R**. Before plantation ends, climb **L** from metal gate towards top of track and along ridge to gate.

❹ After gate, lovely stroll leads across top of Latrigg, with great views of Vale of Keswick, Dodds, Borrowdale, Newlands Valley, and, **R**, massive bulk of Skiddaw.

❺ Beyond highest point of Latrigg, bench is perfectly placed to admire view. From it take path descending gently northwards, keeping **L** then dropping in zig-zags to intercept track alongside another plantation.

❻ At track, turn **L**, and continue down to Spooney Green Lane, which crosses high above A66 and runs on to meet Briar Rigg, back lane. At this junction, turn **L** into Briar Rigg, and follow lane (enclosed path on the **L** along Briar Rigg makes for safer passage), until you can branch **R** at pronounced **L** bend to return to car park.

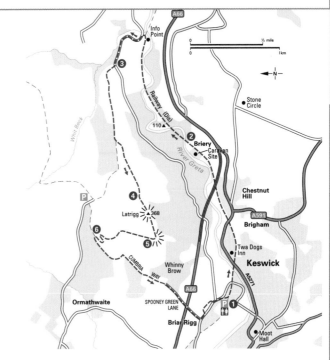

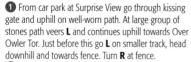

CARL WARK Moorland Ramparts

Tramp along medieval packhorse trails in search of the dwelling place of ancient Britons.

5.5 miles/8.8km 3hrs **Ascent** 328ft/100m ⚠ **Difficulty** 2

Paths Generally good paths

Map OS Explorer OL1 Dark Peak **Grid ref** SK 252801

Parking Surprise View pay car park on A6187 east of Hathersage

❶ From car park at Surprise View go through kissing gate and uphill on well-worn path. At large group of stones path veers **L** and continues uphill towards Over Owler Tor. Just before this go **L** on smaller track, head downhill and towards fence. Turn **R** at fence.

❷ Follow track until it meets dry-stone wall runs parallel with track. Follow path **R** from here past end of large sheepfold. Continue ahead on moorland path. Rocky outcrop of Higger Tor is now on **L** and Carl Wark is ahead **R**.

❸ When path forks, veer **R**. Continue past Carl Wark, keeping it **R**. Go downhill towards the far **R** corner of wood. Cross stone bridge then wooden bridge, head uphill on well-worn path to join old green road and turn **L**.

❹ Continue along track with Burbage Rocks above and **R**. At Upper Burbage Bridge cross 2 streams via large stones, head uphill and follow upper of 2 paths to **L** and uphill. Cross open moorland then ascend

Higger Tor on stone stepped path. Cross tor then descend other side near southeast corner.

❺ Follow track across moor towards Carl Wark. Ascend this and turn **L** to reach summit. After looking around at views return to top of path and, keeping stone ramparts on **L**, descend via path southwards.

❻ From here path heads across boggy section of moor, curves round small, rocky hill then heads downhill towards A6187. Cross on to road via stile, cross road and turn **R** on to pavement.

❼ Turn **L** through gate and down to footbridge. Turn **R** on to Waterside path.

❽ At next footbridge, turn **R** for wide, sunken path between heather. At top, cross road for car park.

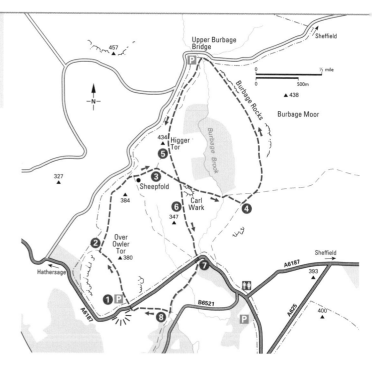

BRADFIELD Dale Dike Dam Disaster

A quiet waterside walk around the site of an horrific industrial tragedy.

5.5 miles/8.8km 3hrs 30min **Ascent** 394ft/120m ⚠ **Difficulty** ①
Paths Minor roads, bridleways, forest paths
Map OS Explorer OL1 Dark Peak **Grid ref** SK 262920
Parking Car park by Low Bradfield cricket ground

❶ Exit car park and turn **R** on to road. At 2nd junction go **R** towards Midhopestones. Follow road uphill passing, on **R**, former inn, Walker House farm and Upper Thornseat. When road turns **R**, with Thomson House below, turn **L** on to overgrown track.

❷ Go through gate in front and on to Hall Lane, public bridleway. Follow along edge of wood then through another gate and go ahead on farm road. Another gate at end of road leads to entrance to Hallfield.

❸ Right of way goes through grounds of Hallfield but alternative permissive path leads **L** through gate, round perimeter of house and through another gate to rejoin bridleway at back of house. Follow bridleway through gate and then past Stubbing Farm.

❹ Next gate leads to Brogging Farm and dam at head of Strines Reservoir. Look for sign near end of farmhouse and turn **L**. Go slightly downhill, over stile, follow path, then cross stile and go through wood.

❺ Cross stream by footbridge, go **R** at junction and straight on at next with stream on **L**. Then follow path along bank of Dale Dike Reservoir to dam head. From here continue through woods, down several sets of steps and continue on path looking out for the memorial to those who were killed in 1864.

❻ Follow path until it reaches road. Cross stile, turn **R** on to road and proceed to road junction. Turn **R**, cross bridge then look for public footpath sign just before entrance to Doe House. Cross stile on **L** and follow path to its end on Mill Lee Road opposite The Plough. Turn **L** and follow road downhill, through village and back to car park.

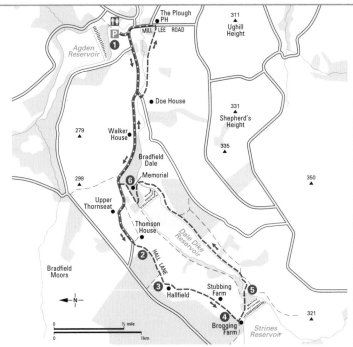

SHIPLEY GLEN A Rural Playground

The playground of the millworkers.

4 miles/6.4km 2hrs **Ascent** 640ft/195m ▲ **Difficulty** 1

Paths Moor and field paths, no stiles

Map OS Explorer 288 Bradford & Huddersfield **Grid ref** SE 131389

Parking On Glen Road, between Bracken Hall Countryside Centre and Old Glen House pub

① Walk down Glen Road, passing Old Glen House pub. Continue as road becomes Prod Lane, signed as a cul-de-sac. Where road ends at entrance to Shipley Glen Tramway, keep ahead to find enclosed path to **R** of house. Follow path, with houses **L**, and woodland **R**. At metal barrier, ignore path to **L**. Keep straight on downhill. 100yds (91m) beyond barrier, at choice of paths bear **L**, contouring steep hillside.

② At fork above building, take **R** branch, which undulates beneath quarried sandstone cliff. When you later come to area of open heath, with panoramic views, take steps, with metal handrails, to cliff top. Turn **R** on path between chain-link fences, which goes around school playing fields, to meet road. Walk **L** along road for 150yds (137m). When level with school on **L**, cross road and take narrow, enclosed path on **R**, between houses. Walk gradually uphill, crossing road in housing estate and picking up enclosed path again. Soon, at kissing gate, you emerge into pasture.

③ Go half **L**, uphill, to kissing gate at the top-**L** corner of field. Head out to join access track along field top to Hope Farm. Walk past buildings on cinder track, leaving just before its end on to bridleway through gate on **R**. Beyond next gate you emerge on Baildon Moor. Path is clear, following wall to **L**. Keep straight on, as wall curves to **L**, towards next farm (and caravan park). Cross metalled farm track and curve **L** to follow boundary wall of Dobrudden Farm.

④ Walk gradually downhill towards Bingley in valley. When wall bears **L**, keep straight ahead, through bracken, more steeply downhill. Cross metalled track and carry on down to meet Glen Road again.

⑤ Follow path along rocky edge of wooded Shipley Glen, leading back to Bracken Hall Countryside Centre and car.

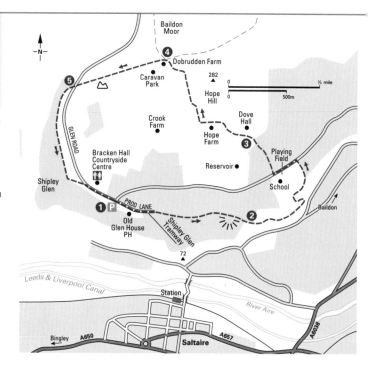

HALIFAX The Shibden Valley
An old packhorse track to a hidden valley.

5 miles/8km 2hrs 30min **Ascent** 1,148ft/350m ⚠ **Difficulty** 1
Paths Old packhorse tracks and field paths, no stiles
Map OS Explorer 288 Bradford & Huddersfield **Grid ref** SE 095254
Parking In Halifax

❶ Walk past tall spire and down Alfred Street and **L** along Church Street, passing smoke-blackened parish church. Bear **L** into Lower Kirkgate, then **R** along Bank Bottom. Cross Hebble Brook and walk uphill; where road bears sharp **L**, keep ahead up steep cobbled lane. At road, go **R** for 200yds (183m). After entrance to a warehouse (Aquaspersion), take cobbled path on **L** for steep ascent up Beacon Hill

❷ This old packhorse track – known as Magna Via – joins another path and continues uphill to large retaining wall and choice of tracks. Keep **L** on a cinder track, slightly downhill. Keep **L** when track forks again; after further 100yds (91m) take walled path on **L**. Drop steeply to pass through housing estate to main road. Cross, beside farm entrance, to path downhill, under railway line into Shibden Park.

❸ Walk to boating lake and bear **L** at sign (Shibden Hall). At next signpost, keep **L** above play area to follow track beside rail embankment. To visit hall go **L**

by pond. Otherwise, take other path signed to car park and facilities. At next junction, go, descending through trees to drive. Climb to gates and turn **R** down Old Godley Lane, which finally swings **L** to main road at Stump Cross.

❹ Cross road and take Staups Lane, to **L** of Stump Cross Inn. Walk along lane to meet another road at top. Go **L** and immediately **L** again down track and through gate to cross fields into Shibden Dale. Emerging at far end on to lane, turn **L** to Shibden Mill Inn.

❺ Pass pub to far end of its car park, where track crosses Shibden Beck. Later, bear **R** at fork and continue to isolated house. Beyond, track narrows to walled path. At houses in Claremount, keep ahead along street that then bends **R** above Godley Cutting to bridge spanning the A58. Over that, steps on **R** drop down to street. Go **L** to its end and retrace route back into Halifax.

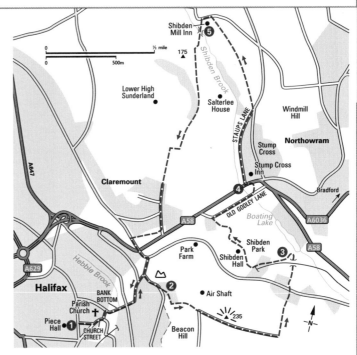

BINGLEY The Druid's Altar
Enjoy great views of Airedale.

6 miles/9.7km 3hrs Ascent 853ft/260m ⚠ **Difficulty** 2
Paths Good paths and tracks throughout, 1 stile
Map OS Explorer 288 Bradford & Huddersfield **Grid ref** SE 107391
Parking Car parks in Bingley

1 Walk downhill from town centre, towards church. Go **L** at traffic lights, passing Old White Horse pub, on to Millgate. Cross River Aire and take the 1st **R**, Ireland Street. Swing immediately **R** and **L** to join riverside track. Bear **R** in front of Ravenroyd Farm, to pass between farm buildings and continue on walled track. Pass house, Cophurst, and continue through pastures beside wood.
2 Leaving trees, ongoing track continues past Marley Farm end over stile and stream on to track by Blakey Cottage. Go **L**, bypassing ford to follow rough track uphill. As it swings into farm, bear **R** on grass trail up bracken-clad slope, arriving at small gate into thicker woodland. Narrow path rises through trees. Bear **R** and then **L** at 2 forks to reach level ground at top of wood beside wall on **R**. After crossing track, path leads to rocky outcrop, Druid's Altar.
3 Bear **R**, after rocks, to meeting of tracks. Go through wall gap opposite, on to walled track into St Ives Estate. Leave immediately through kissing gate on **R** on to

path for 0.5 mile (800m) within Race Course Plantation. Ignore kissing gate at end, go **L**, now descending, through golf course and edge of open heather moor. When accompanying wall turns away, bear **R** with main path, dropping through wood again to reach Lady Blantyre's Rock.
4 Ignore side-tracks, follow path downhill to Coppice Pond. Join metalled road to bear **L** Past Reader's Tea Room, golf clubhouse and on **R** St Ives Mansion.
5 Beyond house, curve **R** and **L** to follow main drive downhill for 0.5 mile (800m). Past car park, take path **L** into woodland. Keep **R** where it forks, to reach B6429, Bingley to Cullingworth road. Cross and continue downhill on Beckfoot Lane. After houses lane becomes unmade track to Beckfoot Farm.
6 Cross bridge and bear L to find allotments on **L**. Where allotments end, take path on **L** to metal footbridge over River Aire and into Myrtle Park. Walk through park to return to Bingley.

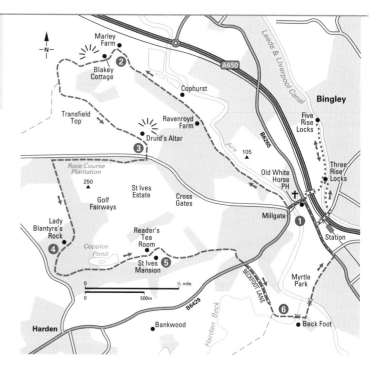

ILKLEY MOOR Twelve Apostles

Discover some ancient standing stones and plenty of history on Ilkley Moor.

4.5 miles/7.2km 2hrs 30min **Ascent** 803ft/245m ⚠️ **Difficulty** ②
Paths Good moorland paths, some steep paths towards end of walk, no stiles
Map OS Explorer 297 Lower Wharfedale **Grid ref** SE 132467
Parking Car park below Cow and Calf rocks

❶ Walk up road; 150yds (137m) beyond Cow and Calf Hotel, where road bears **L**, fork **R** up grassy path. Scramble on to ridge and follow it west past Pancake Stone, enjoying extensive views over Ilkley and Wharfedale. Dip across path rising along shallow gully and continue beyond Haystack Rock, joining another path from **L**. Keep **L** at successive forks, swinging parallel to broad fold containing Backstone Beck, over to **R**.

❷ After gently rising for 0.75 mile (1.2km) across open moor, path eventually meets Bradford–Ilkley Dales Way link. Go **L** here, along section of duckboarding. Pass boundary stone at top of the rise, and continue to ring of stones known as Twelve Apostles, just beyond crest.

❸ Retrace steps from Twelve Apostles, but now continue ahead along Dales Way link. Bear **R** at fork and cross head of Backstone Beck. Shortly, beyond crossing path, way curves **L** in steep, slanting descent

off moor below ridge, levelling lower down as it bends to White Wells.

❹ Turn **R** in front of bathhouse and follow path across slope of hill past small pond and falling below clump of rocks to meet metalled path. Go **R**, taking either branch around The Tarn to find path leaving up steps at end. After crossing Blackstone Beck, ignore rising grass track and continue up final pull to crags by Cow and Calf rocks.

❺ It's worth taking a few minutes to investigate the rocks and watch climbers practising their belays and traverses. From here paved path leads back to car park.

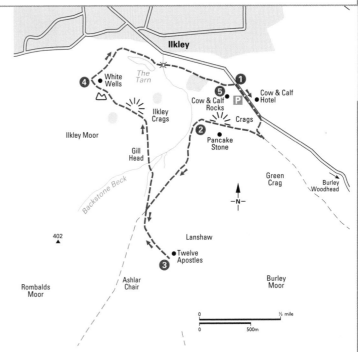

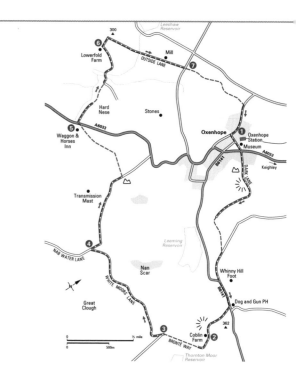

SLAITHWAITE Along The Colne Valley
The rural face of the valley.

6 miles/9.7km 3hrs 30min **Ascent** 550ft/168m ⚠ **Difficulty** 2
Paths Field paths, good tracks and canal towpath, many stiles
Map OS Explorer OL21 South Pennines **Grid ref** SE 079140
Parking Plenty of street parking in Slaithwaite

① Walk along Britannia Road to A62. Cross; walk up Varley Road. After last house go **R**, through stile. Join track across field to stile on **R-H** end of wall ahead. Follow wall to your **R**, across stile, to minor road. Go **R** and follow road **L** to crossroads. Go ahead on track; after 20yds (18m), bear **L** on rack between houses. Squeeze past gate on to field path. Follow wall on **R**; towards end go through gap and take steps in same direction. Follow obvious route down to road.

② Go **R**, along road, for 20yds (18m) and turn **L** on track ('Hollins Lane'). Track becomes rougher; when it peters out, keep **L** of cottage and go through gate. Follow field-edge path ahead, through gates either side of beck. Pass ruined house to descend on walled path. When it bears sharp **R**, keep ahead through gate on to field path. Follow wall on **R**; where it ends keep ahead, across 2 fields, and meet walled track. Go **L**, towards farm. Go **R**, after 50yds (46m), through stile, on to path downhill. It bears **R**; take stile to **L** to follow field-edge path. Cross field, go through kissing gate and turn to walk uphill to path that leads to B6107.

③ Go **R**, on road, for 75yds (69m), and take track to **L**. Keep **L** of house, via gate. 150yds (137m) past house, bear **R** at fork to less obvious track. Soon follow wall. Across beck, track forks; keep **L**, uphill, to skirt shoulder of Hard Hill. Follow track steeply downhill, then up to kissing gate, then down to cross beck on retaining wall. After another climb, it's level Butterley Reservoir ahead. Bear **L**, uphill at tiny building, cross 2 stiles and meet rack. Follow it **R**, downhill, to road.

④ Go **R**, down road, passing houses dwarfed by Bank Bottom Mills. Keep ahead at roundabout, down Fall Lane, soon bearing **L** to dip beneath main road and fork **L** into Marsden. Take Station Road, at far end of green, to Huddersfield Narrow Canal.

⑤ Take path on **R** that joins canal towpath. Follow towpath for 3 miles (4.8km), passing under road, past numerous locks and 2 road bridges into Slaithwaite.

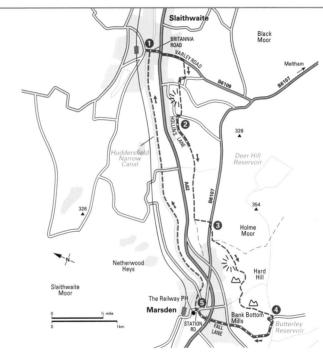

West Yorkshire • NORTHERN ENGLAND

RISHWORTH MOOR Along Blackstone Edge

A bracing ramble on old moorland tracks, with extensive views all the way.

6 miles/9.7km 3hrs **Ascent** 843ft/257m **⚠ Difficulty** ③

Paths Moorland paths; may be boggy after rain, no stiles

Map OS Explorer OL21 South Pennines **Grid ref** SE 010183

Parking Small car park above Baitings Reservoir

❶ From car park, walk 0.5 mile (800m) **L**. Then, 50yds (46m) after crossing beck, take waymarked gate in wall on **R**.

❷ Follow tumbledown wall uphill towards Blackwood Farm. Walk between farmhouse and outbuilding, to gate at top of farmyard. Walk up next field to gate and continue uphill, following wall on **L**. Look for views of Ryburn Valley as you approach crest of hill. Reach ladder stile, next to wall gate.

❸ Don't cross, but strike off **R** over rough moorland; path is distinct but narrow. Occasional yellow-topped markers confirm route, running roughly parallel to M62, aiming to **R** of tall mast on far side of motorway. After 1 mile (1.6km), path begins gentle descent. Keep forward above head of gully then cross plank bridge as path falls across hill to bridge over reservoir drainage channel.

❹ Cross and walk **R**, following watercourse towards reservoir. Ignore next 2 bridges across, but at 3rd, 300yds (274m) before reservoir embankment and waymarked 'Blackstone Edge and Baitings', revert to northern bank. Bear slightly **L** to follow path uphill before it levels and swings **L** around Flint Hill. It later curves **R** to crest watershed into Upper Ryburn Valley at junction of paths by water channel.

❺ Go **R** (sign to Baitings Reservoir), continuing to skirt hill on level path. After 1 mile (1.6km), watch for fork marked by wooden post and bear **L**, gradually descending towards Baitings Reservoir. At wall corner, keep ahead, following wall on **L**. Soon on walled track, pass through 3 gates and emerging at car park at start.

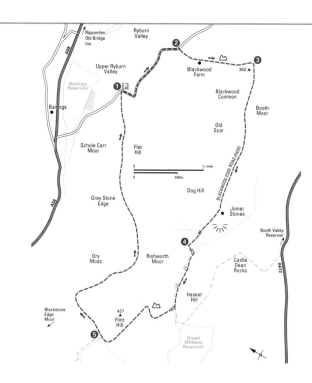

HARDCASTLE CRAGS Two Wooded Valleys

Walk in a pair of beautiful wooded valleys, linked by a high level path.

5 miles/8km 2hrs 30min **Ascent** 935ft/285m ⚠ **Difficulty** 2
Paths Good paths and tracks, plus open pasture, no stiles
Map OS Explorer OL21 South Pennines **Grid ref** SD 987293 **Parking** National Trust pay-and-display car parks at Midgehole, near Hebden Bridge (accessible via A6033, Keighley Road)

❶ From non-member car park at Midgehole, walk back to main drive. Go **L** towards lodge but, just past information board, double back **R** on path falling to picnic area beside river. Keep **L** at any choice of paths and continue upstream for 1 mile (1.6km) to reach Gibson Mill, occasionally climbing above river where it becomes constricted between rocky banks.

❷ Join main drive to follow it beyond mill, soon passing crags that give woods their name. Keep **R** at later fork, shortly emerging from trees and National Trust estate to join rough metalled drive. It runs **L** at farm and adjacent cottages at Walshaw.

❸ Just before houses –opposite barns – turn sharp **R** through gate on to enclosed track (signed 'Crimsworth Dean'). Running on as field track, it peters out beyond another gate to follow wall over shoulder of Shackleton Knoll. Approaching watershed, path slips through gate to continue on wall's opposite flank. Developing as track, it later turns through another gate and drops into Crimsworth Dean, ending at junction

beside ruin of Nook Farm. Along length of valley, rough way is old road from Hebden Bridge to Howarth and is great walk for another day.

❹ For now, turn **R** along this elevated track, passing farm on **L**. Make short detour **R** at next fork to see Abel Cross, pair of old waymarker stones standing beside track. Return to main track and continue down valley, soon re-entering woodland of National Trust estate. Keep **L** at successive forks, eventually returning to car parks at Midgehole.

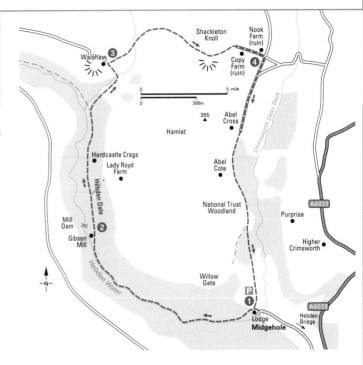

MUSTON Gristhorpe Man
Where prehistoric man lived and died.

3.75 miles/6km 2hrs **Ascent** 249ft/75m ▲ **Difficulty** 1
Paths Field paths and tracks, muddy after rain, 4 stiles
Map OS Explorer 301 Scarborough, Bridlington & Flamborough Head **Grid ref** TA 096796
Parking Street parking in Muston, near the Ship Inn

❶ From Ship Inn, walk in direction of Folkton. After houses end, and just before stone holding Muston village sign on **R**, take waymarked stile in hedge on **L**, signed 'Wolds Way'. Go forward with hedge on **R**. Path becomes track. Follow Wolds Way signs uphill over 2 waymarked stiles, passing 2 disused stiles on ascent. At top **R-H** corner of next field cross stile and continue ahead to next signpost.

❷ Go over embankment then turn **R** down track, following bridleway sign. Continue downhill, on this hollow way. It comes into field, which you walk straight across to reach main road, Flotmanby Lane.

❸ Cross road and walk through farm buildings of Manor Farm, bearing **R** along track by barn. Track eventually bears **L** and crosses stream, then reaches drainage channel that is crossed by concrete bridge with metal rails.

❹ Cross bridge and turn **R** at end, along side of channel. Follow track to next bridge. Do not cross, but continue ahead, still following channel. Go through waymarked gate and continue ahead; drainage channel eventually swings **R**, away from path. Continue through 2 more waymarked gates.

❺ Before you reach another waymarked gate, turn **L**. Walk up field side with hedge on **R**. Follow hedge as it bends round to **R**. Path reaches waymarked gate. Go through gate into track (Carr Lane).

❻ Follow Carr Lane between hedges and past farm buildings. Eventually lane becomes metalled and passes houses to reach T-junction before green.

❼ Turn **R**, then **R** again at main road. Follow main street of Muston as it winds through village, past All Saints Church, to Ship Inn.

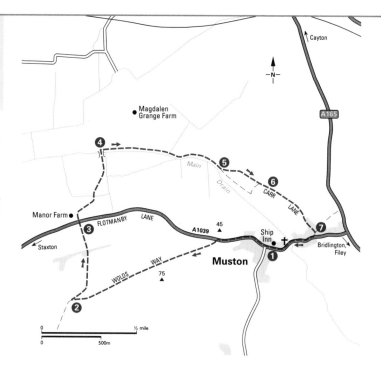

SCARBOROUGH Through Raincliffe Woods

A woodland walk to a glacial lake.

5 miles/8km 2hrs **Ascent** 584ft/178m ⚠ **Difficulty** 2
Paths Field tracks, woodland paths, some steep, 2 stiles
Map OS Explorer OL 27 North York Moors – Eastern **Grid ref** SE 984875
Parking Car park on Low Road, near road junction

❶ From car park, turn **L** on road, then **R** at junction. Go downhill, and after woodland ends, pass houses on **R**. Opposite bungalow, No. 5, turn **R** down track to Thorn Park Farm. Follow track as it bends **L** by farm buildings, then **R** past cottage to metal gate. Continue on track, which bends **L**, **R**, then through 2 gateways.
❷ Just before next gateway, turn **R** and walk up field side to go through gateway, which takes you on short path to road. Turn **L**, follow road and continue to next car park on **R**.
❸ Go through car park, bearing **L** toward signboard, then go uphill on path ahead. Where main path bends **R**, go straight ahead, more steeply, to crossing, grassy track. Turn **L** and follow path. Where it forks, take **R-H** path.
❹ After 500yds (457m) look for faint path on **L**, which immediately bends **R** over drainage runnel. Path goes down into small valley. Turn **L**, downhill, then

follow now-obvious path as it bends **R** again, past old quarry. Path descends to reach Throxenby Mere. Turn **R** along edge of Mere now on boardwalks.
❺ Just before you reach picnic place, go through gate and immediately turn **R**. Follow path which goes up steeply, ignoring all joining paths until it reaches track at hill top.
❻ Turn **R** and go beside metal gate, then follow path for 1 mile (1.6km), parallel with 1st fence and then wall. It passes through gateway with stile beside and eventually reaches gate with public bridleway sign.
❼ Ignore gate into fields, but turn **R** and continue beside wire fence on edge of woodland. Where main path swings **L** and another goes **R**, go straight ahead, steeply downhill. When path joins another go **L**, down steps and along boardwalk to meet crossing path.
❽ Turn **R** and follow path, which soon descends to car park at start.

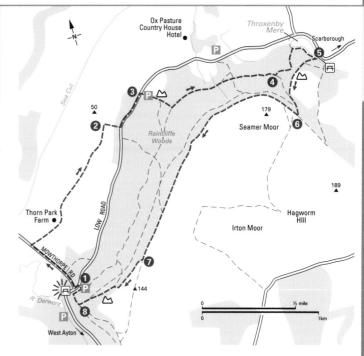

ROBIN HOOD'S BAY Along The Coast
Along part of the Cleveland Way.

5.5 miles/8.8km 2hrs 30min **Ascent** 466ft/142m ⚠ **Difficulty** 1
Paths Field and coastal paths, a little road walking, 4 stiles
Map OS Explorer OL 27 North York Moors – Eastern **Grid ref** NZ 950055
Parking Car park at top of hill into Robin Hood's Bay, by the old railway station

❶ From the car park, take entry road to main road. Turn **L** up hill out of village. Just after road bends round to **L**, take signed footpath to **R** over stile. Walk up fields over 3 stiles to metalled lane.
❷ Turn **R**. Go **L** through signed metal gate. At end of field path bends **R** to waymarked gate in hedge on **L**. Continue down next field with stone wall on **L**. Again, go **R** at field end and over stile into green lane.
❸ Cross to another waymarked stile and continue along field edge with wall on **R**. At field end, go over stile on **R**, then make for waymarked gate diagonally **L**.
❹ Walk towards farm, through gate and take waymarked track through farmyard. Continue with stone wall on **R**, through another gate and on to track that bends **L** to waymarked stile.
❺ Continue to stile before footbridge over beck. Cross bridge, then bear **R** across hedge line, following waymarker, then diagonally **R** towards next waymarker and signpost for Hawsker. Cross stream and bear **R**. As

hedge to **R** curves **L**, go through gap on **R** and over signed stile, walking ahead through field to another stile on to main road.
❻ Go **R** and **R** again, following footpath sign, up metalled lane. Pass Seaview Holiday Park, cross former railway track and continue along metalled lane, which bends **R**, goes downhill, crosses stream and ascends to Northcliffe Holiday Park.
❼ Follow Robin Hood's Bay sign **R**, and follow metalled road, bending **L** beside gate and down through caravans. Beyond them, leave track to bear **L** to waymarked path. Follow path towards coastline, to reach signpost.
❽ Turn **R** along Cleveland Way for 2.5 miles (4km). Footpath goes through kissing gate and over 3 stiles, then through 2 more kissing gates. It passes through Rocket Post Field by 2 more gates. Continue on path past houses and ahead along road to main road. Car park is opposite.

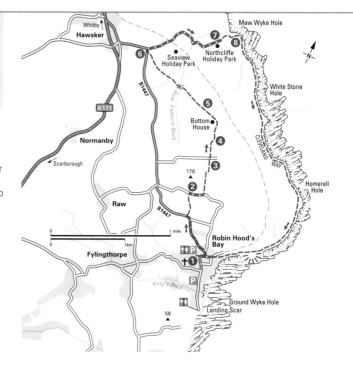

FYLINGDALES A Forest Trail

Visit the early-warning system at Fylingdales and Lilla Cross.

6.75 miles/10.9km 3hrs **Ascent** 642ft/196m ⚠ **Difficulty** 1

Paths Forest tracks and moorland paths, 3 stiles
Map OS Explorer OL 27 North York Moors – Eastern **Grid ref** SX 106836
Parking May Beck car park, beside stream

❶ Walk up wide track opposite approach road. Where track bends to **R**, go **L** down signed footpath and descend to go over bridge and bear **R** to continue along green track. Go through kissing gate and up valley, eventually swinging away from stream and into forest.

❷ At forest road turn **R**, passing flooded quarry on **R**. At next junction of forest roads bear **R**. After about 0.25 mile (400m), turn up track to **L**.

❸ Go up track, leaving forest for moorland. Continue past base and shaft of York Cross. At track going **L**, near waymarked post, turn sharp **L**.

❹ Walk along track, bearing **L** at Foster Howes tumuli, and continue with fence on **R**. Pass Ann's Cross to **R** and 0.5 mile (800m) beyond reach T-junction. Turn **R** through gate and take track to **L**.

❺ At crossroads with signpost, turn **R** along track to visit Lilla Cross. Return to crossroads, and go straight ahead, following Robin Hood's Bay sign. Follow path, which goes parallel with forest edge, for 2.5 miles

(4km), eventually heading for lone tree to **R** of wood's end.

❻ Bear **R** at post with number 9 on it. Pass posts 8 and 7, going **L** at trail sign.

❼ Pass post 6, (by the remains of John Cross) and go through gate, to continue downhill on track. After 50yds (46m), go **L** off track and walk parallel with woodland to waymarked stile near ruins of building.

❽ Go to **L** of building and ahead to another stile. Follow obvious footpath downhill through bracken, passing 2 public footpath signs, to road. Turn **L** to return to start.

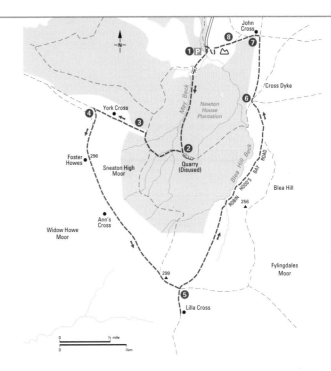

65

THIRSK Herriot's Darrowby

James Herriot based his fictional home town on his real one – Thirsk.

5 miles/8km 2hrs **Ascent** 66ft/20m ⚠ **Difficulty** 1

Paths Town paths, field paths and tracks, 6 stiles

Map OS Explorer 302 Northallerton & Thirsk **Grid ref** SE 430813

Parking Roadside parking in the main street of Sowerby village

❶ Walk down street, away from Thirsk. Just past Methodist Church on **L**, go **L** on Blakey Lane. Cross bridge, turn **L** on signed path and follow stream, going through 2 kissing gates to footbridge.

❷ Continue beside stream to stile. Go through 2 gates to car park and ahead to road. Cross and take path that curves **L**, then **R** by bridge. At paved area, turn **R** to go alongside green to road.

❸ Cross road and continue ahead, crossing main road and going **L** at top of green. Cross metal bridge and continue beside beck by church. Before road take path to **R**, beside bench, to footbridge on **R**.

❹ Cross bridge and go ahead through 2 gates, curving **L** to follow beck to gate by bridge. Go ahead (not over bridge) and follow path across fields, veering diagonally **R** to stile on **R**.

❺ Over stile follow stream, crossing 2 stiles to pass beside houses. Continue **L** over footbridge by mill buildings. Path winds **R** to cross 2nd footbridge. Follow bridleway sign across field through gate to main road.

❻ Cross road and go through signed gate opposite, to 2nd gate beside wood. 150yds (137m) after wood, turn **L** at waymark.

❼ Walk down field with hedge **L**. In 2nd field, go **L** over stile and continue with hedge **R**, bearing half **L** to another stile. Continue over field, then down next field edge, bearing **L**, then **R** at end to path that becomes lane between hedges.

❽ At road go ahead, bearing **L**, then **R** past church. Turn **R** and walk into town centre. In Market Place, cross by clock tower towards Golden Fleece. Go down signed passageway 2 premises to **L** of pub, cross lane and go down Villa Place.

❾ Bear **L** to pass swimming pool. Turn **R** and bend round pool building to gate. Go ahead to gate and parallel with beck. At bridge, turn **R** across field on track to gate on to lane, then ahead back to Sowerby.

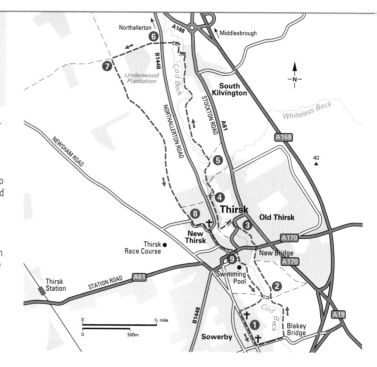

HUBBERHOLME Dalesfolk Traditions

From J B Priestley's favourite Dales village, along Langstrothdale.

5.25 miles/8.4km 2hrs **Ascent** 480ft/146m ⚠ **Difficulty** 2
Paths Field paths and tracks, steep after Yockenthwaite, 11 stiles
Map OS Explorer OL 30 Yorkshire Dales – Northern & Central **Grid ref** SD 927782
Parking Beside river in village, opposite church (not church parking)

❶ Enter farmyard beside church and turn **L** immediately through Dales Way signed gate. Take lower path, signed 'Yockenthwaite', alongside churchyard. Walk beside river for 1.25 miles (2km); clear Dales Way path is never far from river. Approaching Yockenthwaite, go up steps to little gate and **L** to gate and signpost.

❷ Follow track towards bridge but, before it, go sharp **R** up farm track, which swings back **L** to sign to Cray and Hubberholme.

❸ Go up to another signpost, then follow obvious track slanting **R** and up. Part-way up hill, go **R** at footpath sign through gate.

❹ Follow near-level path to signpost, then bear **L** and up rough section to another signpost. Turn **R** and follow obvious path, descending very gently along beautiful natural terrace until path goes **L** and up to enter wood by footbridge over miniature gorge.

❺ Walk through wood then continue, level again, to small side valley above house. Signpost above house

points towards Cray. Go up slightly, over rocks, then along another green terrace path for 1 mile (1.6km) to footbridge. Cross, then ascend slightly to barn; bear **R** to gate then follow marked path across meadow land. Pass house to junction of tracks on edge of Cray.

❻ Go sharp **R**, down to footpath sign to Stubbing Bridge. Descend between walls and through gate and on to grassy hillside. Pass another footpath sign and continue downhill to meet stream.

❼ Follow streamside path past waterfalls and pools, crossing bridge over side-stream. Cross stile and continue past barn to reach road. Turn **R** back to parking place in Hubberholme.

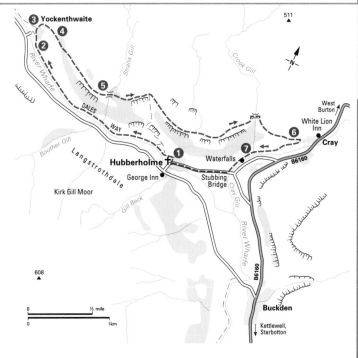

MASHAM A Druidic Dream

A rural ramble from a mock-druidic temple.

4.25 miles/6.8km 2hrs **Ascent** 426ft/130m ⚠ **Difficulty** 1

Paths Tracks and field paths, 7 stiles
Map OS Explorer 298 Nidderdale **Grid ref** SE 177787
Parking Car park by Druid's Temple

❶ Walk down road you drove up. Just after row of metal posts, cross stile on **L** marked with Ripon Rowel Walk symbol, opposite farm track. Walk ahead across field and go though gate surrounded by boulders. Bend **L**, along wood edge and at farm track, go **L** to gate.

❷ After gate turn **R**, following track. It bends away from wood and down to ladder stile. After stile, bear half **L** across field towards pine trees to stile in crossing wire fence. Continue ahead, bearing slightly **L**, to descend by small wood to 2 stout wooden posts, one of them waymarked.

❸ At posts turn sharp **R**, uphill, on grassy track. Follow rutted track, mostly level, until it passes to **R** of Broadmires farm. Track becomes stony and then leads straight out into metalled lane. At road junction continue ahead, now descending. On bend, turn **R** through metal gate towards Stonefold farm.

❹ Walk past farmhouse, then turn **L** through gate into small enclosure. Cross stile and go few paces to another stile. Now bear **R** to gate then continue ahead to waymarked post. Bear **R** across field through gateway in crossing fence and pick up descending track, which bears **R**. Below plantation, leave track and cross stile on **L**. Follow narrow path to another stile and footbridge just beyond.

❺ Cross bridge and waymarked stile, then turn **R**, along track. Go through 2 gates, past barn, and through another metal gate on to lane.

❻ Turn **L**, then **R** on next track. Go over stile beside gate, and along track. After gateway, turn **R** alongside wall, climbing toward farm on ridge. Approaching farm, cross stile in wire fence.

❼ After stile, bend to **L**, following wooden fence, in front of farm building then through metal gate on **R-H** side. Follow farm track and exit onto metalled lane over stile by gate. Turn **L** back to start.

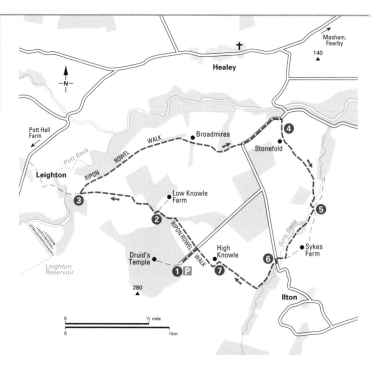

BORDLEY The Monks' Road

A walk around remote farmsteads and on an old walled green lane, with monastic origins, between Malhamdale and Wharfedale.

5 miles/8km 2hrs **Ascent** 436ft/133m ⚠ **Difficulty** ☐1

Paths Tracks and field paths, 2 stiles **Map** OS Explorer OL2 Yorkshire Dales – Southern & Western

Grid ref SD 952653 **Parking** Roadside parking, where lane reaches open moor

❶ From parking place go through gate and follow metalled lane downhill to crossroad of tracks. Turn **R**, on to track signposted 'Kilnsey'. Follow track parallel with dry-stone wall on **R** to reach crossing track at another signpost. This is Mastiles Gate.

❷ Turn **L** along lane signed 'Street Gate'. Follow lane for 1 mile (1.6km), climbing gently and then descending between walls into shallow valley. Go through gate and continue for 100yds (91m) to gate on the **L** from which rough track heads down to ford stream. Follow rough track across stream, over slight rise and across rough pasture.

❸ Eventually it runs between walls, bearing **R** near large triangular boulder. Continue down to meet metalled lane and turn **L** to Middle Laithe. Walk through farmyard and over cattle grid. Follow farm track, crossing cattle grid by National Trust sign for New House farm.

❹ Continue into walled lane which leads into farmyard of New House. Bear **R** through gate then bear **L** down field to gate in bottom **L-H** corner. Go through gate, turn **L** and follow telegraph poles. Cross stile and descend across stream.

❺ Climb away from stream and bear **R**, then contour around hillside. Path meets and follows wall on **R**. Go through first gate on **R** and follow wall on **L**, bearing **R** to go through gap in crossing wall.

❻ Turn **L** to go round angle of wall on **L** to stone stile in crossing wall. Follow wall on **L** up field, past tumbled wall, to join track.

❼ Turn **R** along track and continue to gate just above Bordley. Drop down **R**, then double back **L** to pass **R** of 1st stone barn to double gates. Beyond gates turn **R** and follow track past farmhouse. Climb metalled lane, which reverts to rough track as it levels out. Descend to crossroads and turn **R** to ascend hill back to start.

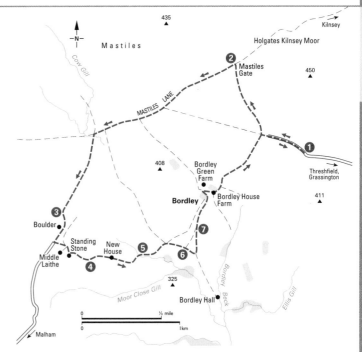

BOLTON ABBEY River And Woodland
Over moorland and alongside the Strid to the romantic priory.

6.75 miles/10.9km 2hrs 30min **Ascent** 870ft/265m ⚠ **Difficulty** ②
Paths Field and moorland paths, then riverside tracks, 3 stiles
Map OS Explorer OL2 Yorkshire Dales – Southern & Western **Grid ref** SE 071539
Parking Main pay-and-display car park at Bolton Abbey

❶ Leave car park at north end, by Village Store. Turn **R** and walk to B6160. Turn **L** and follow road under archway. Opposite battlemented Bolton Hall, turn **L** on a signed track. At top of track, go through gate on **R** with bridleway sign. Walk under power line to signpost. Pass 2 pools to gate, then bear **R** to another gate into woodland.

❷ Follow rising track through wood, with several signs, to another gate. Follow blue waymarks, most painted on rocks, across fields. At crest bear **L** to gate in corner, then turn **L** along wall. Path climbs more steeply onto Hare Head. Descend gently to gate, and 20yds (18m) beyond, take path downhill, trending **R** lower down, to signpost.

❸ Turn **R** on path, parallel to road, to signpost 'FP to B6160'. Follow track to stile, then take **L** fork, going roughly level across moor, to wall corner. Continue to next wall, then turn **R** along it, following improving track to signpost.

❹ Turn **L** over stile and follow wall down to road. Turn **R** a few paces then enter car park. Pass beside Strid Wood Visitor Centre and follow tracks, signed 'The Strid', down to river close to its narrowest part at Strid.

❺ Follow wide tracks downstream to information board and gateway near Cavendish Pavilion. Bear **L** by café and cross footbridge.

❻ Immediately after bridge turn **R**, signed 'Bolton Abbey'. Path briefly joins vehicle track to cross side-stream then bears **R**. When path forks, take either branch (higher has better views of priory). Descend to bridge beside stepping-stones near priory.

❼ Cross bridge and walk straight on. Climb steps to gateway – Hole in the Wall. Go through to road, **L** few paces, then **R** to car park.

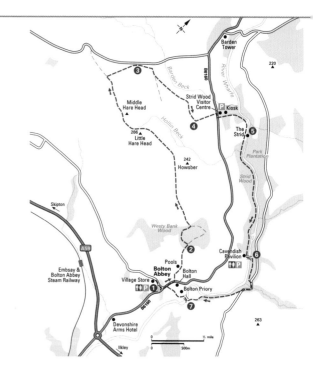

LOTHERSDALE Tucked Away Village

A short walk with fine views and a glimpse of Lothersdale's industrial past.

4 miles/6.4km 2hrs **Ascent** 1,509ft/460m ⚠ **Difficulty** 2
Paths Tracks and field paths, some steep sections. 8 stiles
Map OS Explorer OL21 South Pennines **Grid ref** SD 939472
Parking Roadside parking on Carleton to Colne road, north of Clogger Lane

❶ From car park walk downhill towards mast on next hilltop. Just before cattle grid, turn **L** up signed track. At next signpost turn **R**, off track. Follow wall, then bear **L** to cut off corner as it bends **L**. Soon cross stile in wall on **R**. Bear **L**, above small plantation, then go diagonally **R**. Go over stile and continue downhill with wall **R**, which bends **L** to reach signed stile on to metalled drive.

❷ Turn **L** along drive. After cattle grid, bear **R** along concrete road and over another cattle grid. Emerge on to metalled lane and turn **L**. Follow lane as it dips to cross small stream, then immediately turn **R**.

❸ Follow track, which bends **L** below house, then continues across field with wall on **L**. From next gate bear **R** to another gate and continue down, following wall on **L** towards pool in valley. Cross stile in corner, turn **L** immediately through gate and in few paces go **L** and up to join track. Turn **R** and follow it to road. Turn **L**. Just beyond Hare and Hounds pub, turn **L** at Pennine Way sign.

❹ Follow track uphill to Pennine Way sign. Turn **L** here to follow fence and then wall on **L**, crossing small stream. Continue ahead to stile beside gate on **L**, signed with acorn. Go straight across field to stone stile on to lane.

❺ Cross lane and continue up track ahead, signed 'Pennine Way'. Where concrete farm track bends **L**, go ahead over stone stile on to walled track. Where walls open out, follow one on **L** to stile, then continue following wall on **L** to where it bends sharply **L**.

❻ Follow wall **L**, go over 2 plank bridges and continue along well-worn path, past occasional cairns to trig point on hilltop. Follow either of 2 downhill paths, which soon rejoin, and continue past signpost you passed near start of walk. Continue downhill to road and turn **R** return to start.

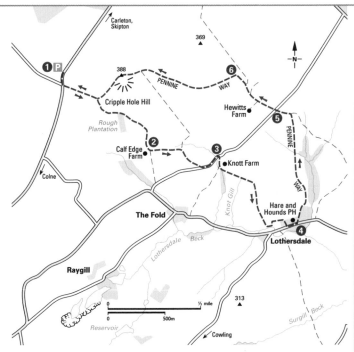

North Yorkshire • NORTHERN ENGLAND

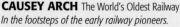

CAUSEY ARCH The World's Oldest Railway

In the footsteps of the early railway pioneers.

4 miles/6.4km 2hrs **Ascent** 394ft/120m ⚠ **Difficulty** 2
Paths Mostly on tracks, one short stiff climb
Map OS Explorer 308 Durham & Sunderland **Grid ref** NZ 205561
Parking Causey Arch car park, off A6076

① From car park, walk through 'Exit' archway. Cross road and take signed footpath, to **L** of bus stop. Cross stile and go up field to cross stile on to metalled road.
② Turn **L**. After 100yds (91m) turn **R**, signed 'Beamish Hall'. Where concrete track swings **R**, go straight ahead down footpath, which leads to farm track. Go ahead. Where track forks, bend **R**. Eventually track goes through gateway and into woodland.
③ Descend between houses to road, opposite Beamish Hall. Turn **R** and follow road for 0.5 mile (800m) to entrance, on **L**, to Beamishburn Picnic Area. Turn **L** and follow lane through picnic site to footbridge.
④ Cross bridge and follow footpath which bends **R**. Where path forks continue along burn side and at bench turn **L** up steps and go **R** at wide crossing track to road. Turn **L** and then go **R**, by Mole Hill Farm sign.
⑤ Go through wooden stile beside gate. Climb track to yellow waymark sign on post. Go **L** off track, and

follow path over wooden stile. Continue with hedge on **R** to another stile. Path beyond curves downhill to road.
⑥ Cross road and take footpath opposite. Ascend hill, cross field and descend to another road. Turn **R** on road for 0.5 mile (800m) to 'Tanfield Railway' sign.
⑦ Turn **R**, up approach road, then go ahead through fence gap. Follow wagon track alongside burn, above gorge, and eventually climb steps to bench by start of Causey Arch. To avoid descent into valley, cross arch and continue along path back to car park.
⑧ To view arch, turn **L** at bench and go downhill, crossing burn on footbridge. Follow path through woodland and over another footbridge. Go **R** at end, then cross another footbridge by quarry. Do not cross next footbridge, but bear **R**, up steps. Turn **L** at top and follow embankment back to car park.

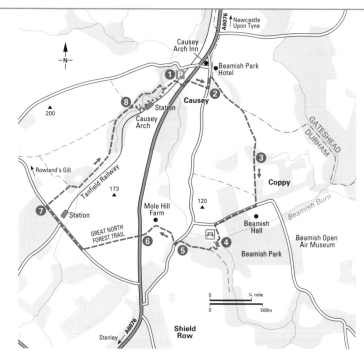

CONSETT A Steel Walk

A walk through the banks of the river that first brought steel making to Consett, with plenty of industrial relics.

4 miles/6.4km 1hr 45min **Ascent** 311ft/95m ⚠ **Difficulty** 1️⃣

Paths River and streamside paths with some roadside walking
Map OS Explorer 307 Consett & Derwent Reservoir **Grid ref** NZ 088522
Parking Roadside parking on Shotley Grove Road off A691

1 From parking area, take steps down to footbridge and cross River Derwent. Walk upstream along tree-lined path, ignoring turnings **R** as it meanders between riverside meadows and Derwent. Pass another bridge and, where path divides, stay by river. Eventually reach beech woodland where path rises on to wider track.

2 Follow track, keeping **L** when it forks – waymarks on this section. Path follows wire fence, and eventually bears **R** over tiny stone bridge skirting house to reach A68.

3 Turn **L** down hill. Go over road bridge, passing from Northumberland into Durham. Where road joins from **L**, go **L** through entrance into Allensford Country Park. Bear **R**, and walk through grassed riverside area to car park. Go through car park to road by caravan site entrance.

4 Cross road to stile marked 'Derwentside Local Nature Reserve Allensford Wood'. Follow path, which goes up 2 sets of steps. At top follow grassy path. Where it divides, bear **L** and follow winding path into woodland and continue downhill. At crossing path, turn **L** to road.

5 Turn **R** and follow road (take care – it can be busy). It rises through woodland, then passes through more open area. After 0.5 mile (800m), pass road **R**. In 0.25 mile (400m) look for footpath that descends on **R** to meet road, by trees.

6 Continue to follow road for 400yds (366m). As roads rises, take signed footpath **L**, downhill into woodland. Path opens out into track, then becomes path again. Follow path for 0.5 mile (800m) to lane. Turn **L** here, downhill. Continue down lane, passing Grove House **L** to reach parking area.

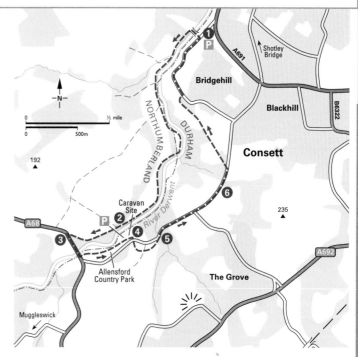

WESTGATE Through Meadow And Woodland

Visit Weardale's prettiest village and stride high above the land of the Prince Bishops.

6.75 miles/10.9km 4hrs **Ascent** 525ft/160m ⚠ **Difficulty** ②

Paths Field paths, tracks and country lanes, 5 stiles
Map OS Explorer OL31 North Pennines **Grid ref** NY 909380
Parking By river at Westgate

❶ From car park walk out to road bridge over River Wear. Don't cross, but follow path on **L**, down steps, then into fields ahead, alongside river's south bank. Path crosses minor road close to ford and footbridge, then continues by cottages and across riverside meadows, passing cottages at Windyside.

❷ On reaching main road at Daddry Shield, cross road and crash barrier on far side to continue down to Wear's south bank again. Path stays closer to river than before. Turn **L** on meeting country lane and follow it into village of St John's Chapel. Turn **R** along main street and pass through village.

❸ At the far side of village, turn **R** along signed footpath that tucks under old railway bridge and crosses footbridge over river. Beyond bridge turn **L** and follow enclosed track past house. Turn **L** through yard, emerging at kissing gate on far side by river, following path close to north bank. Ignore next footbridge, but instead head for farmhouse, which

should be rounded on **L**.

❹ Follow grassy enclosed path raking diagonally across hillside pasture to reach high country lane above New House.

❺ Turn **R** along lane (3rd **R** of those available) then, after 0.75 mile (1.2km), take higher **L-H** fork which traverses southern side of Carr Brow Moor with its disused quarries and mine shafts.

❻ At terminus turn **L** up walled Seeingsike Road (track). Turn **R** at junction of tracks and descend into Middlehope Cleugh. Convenient stones allow crossing of river, though if it is in spate retrace your steps to Point ❻ and find different way into Westgate.

❼ Turn **R** again to follow Middlehope Burn's east bank, past lead mines. Path enters Slit Woods and comes out by mill and cottages on edge of Westgate.

❽ Lane leads to main road where you turn **L**, then **R** past Hare and Hounds pub, back to car park.

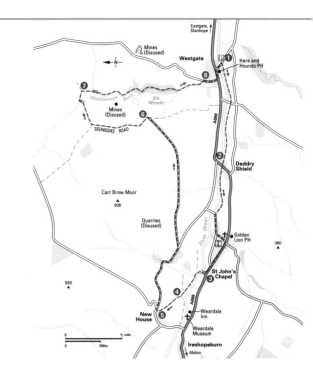

ROOKHOPE Industrial Land

Among the relics of the lead-mining industry.

5.25 miles/8.4km 2hrs **Ascent** 508ft/155m ⚠ **Difficulty** 2

Paths Tracks and field paths, one steep climb. Use former railway tracks as embankment may be unstable in places **Map** OS Explorer 307 Consett & Derwent Reservoir **Grid ref** NY 924430

Parking Parking area beside Rookhope Arch, west of village

❶ Walk toward Rookhope. Opposite Blanchland road go **R**, over stile and footbridge. Go ahead, bending **L** after white building, then **R** on track. Go through gate, and **L**, uphill. After cattle grid bear **L** when track divides. Go through 2 metal gates to white house.

❷ Beyond, take path **L**; descend, go through gate in wall **R**. Cross field to stile, then through gate to stile by farm buildings. Pass in front of them to wooden stile. Head downhill towards village, to ladder stile.

❸ After stile, walk past buildings and turn **R** along track for 0.75 mile (1.2km), going through 3 gates, then through farmyard with 2 more. Follow track beyond, uphill, to where it bends **L**.

❹ Turn **L**. As track disappears, continue down to stile. Turn **L** along road. Just after lay-by, go **R** over stile, signed 'Weardale Way'. Cross footbridge and climb path opposite, bearing **R**. Walk through field, go over stile, then uphill to stile on ridge.

❺ Cross lane and go through kissing gate. Stay on **R-H** side up field, but in next field, on approaching old mine spoil, aim off **L** towards gate by static caravan next to farmhouse. Continue between house and barn to kissing gate on far side of yard.

❻ Cross next field in line with transmission poles. At next buildings – Chestergarth House– go though gate and bear **R**, along back of farm to pair of gates on far side by shed. Take **L-H** gate and walk out into field beyond communications mast. Now drop steeply down to bottom **R** corner of field to meet road. Turn **R**, then **R** again at junction into Rookhope.

❼ Pass post office and Rookhope Inn, then take signed path, **L**. Cross bridge and turn **R** along track at 'Rookhope Trails' sign. Path ascends to higher track. Continue over stile and ahead, past nursery. After gate and wooden stile, turn **R** over footbridge, go over stile and turn **L** on road to return to start.

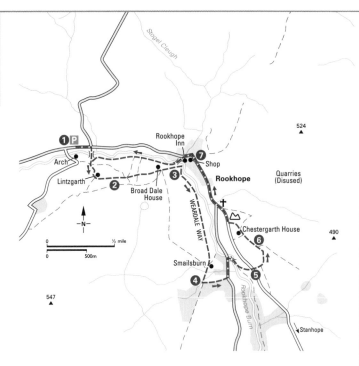

COW GREEN Reservoir And The Tees
The remote hillscapes of Widdybank Fell.

8 miles/12.9km 5hrs **Ascent** 525ft/160m **⚠ Difficulty** ③
Paths Roads tracks and well-defined paths, one short scramble, 2 stiles
Map OS Explorer OL31 North Pennines **Grid ref** NY 810309
Parking Car park at Cow Green

❶ From car park walk back along road across desolate Widdybank Fell and over watershed. Go ahead at junction with Harwood road.

❷ As road approaches river, leave it for signposted path on **R**, which follows track to Widdybank Farm. Winding track heads for rocks of Cronkley Scar, which lies on far banks of River Tees.

❸ Through farmyard of Widdybank path goes over stile by gate and veers **L** across rough pasture to join Pennine Way by banks of Tees.

❹ Across grassy plains at first, path threads through tightening gorge, eventually squeezed by cliffs and boulders of Falcon Clints on to bouldery course close to river. Briefly grassy plain develops and path, sometimes stony and traversing heather and sometimes crossing marshy areas using duckboards, continues into wild North Pennine recesses. Across river warning signs are posted by the army to keep you

from straying on to their firing range. Usually the guns are a long way off and all is calm.

❺ Valley of Maize Beck comes in from behind Black Hill in west, and route comes to foot of impressive cataract of Cauldron Snout. Here path becomes a scramble up rocks beside falls – take care.

❻ At top of falls is huge Cow Green dam. Here Pennine Way turns **L** to cross footbridge over Tees, but route continues along lane, which climbs to top **R** of dam.

❼ Lane continues above eastern shores of reservoir. Now on nature trail and there are numbered attractions but no interpretation notices (explanatory leaflet available from local TICs). Beyond gate across road leave tarmac and turn **L** along track to car park.

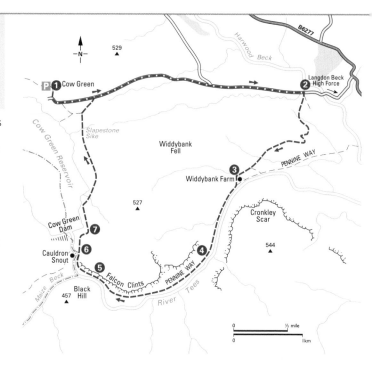

BARNARD CASTLE Around Old Barney

A town and riverside walk with plenty of history.

4.25 miles/6.8km 2hrs 30min **Ascent** 165ft/50m ⚠ **Difficulty** ☐ 1
Paths Town streets and good paths, 6 stiles
Map OS Explorer OL31 North Pennines **Grid ref** NZ 051163
Parking Pay-and-display car park at end of Queen Street between Galgate and Newgate

❶ From car park go through passageway signposted for river. Go across Newgate Street and continue through another ginnel, which leads through churchyard of St Mary's, then out on to riverside parkland of Demesnes.

❷ Here turn **L** along stony path, which angles down to river. It passes Demesnes Mill, then follows north bank of Tees, with river **R**.

❸ Pass (quickly if wind is in wrong direction) sewage works. Ignore upper **L** fork of 2 paths and stay by river to enter pretty woodland, which allows glimpses of remains of Egglestone Abbey on far banks. Go through gate on to road and turn **R** over Abbey Bridge.

❹ Turn **R** at junction on far side of bridge, then go **L** up access track to view abbey. Return to road and follow it **L**, to pass Bow Bridge. Squeeze stile in hedge on **R** marks start of path along south bank of Tees. On approach to caravan park path crosses fields and veers slightly away from river.

❺ Turn **R** along surfaced track, down to caravan park and take 2nd drive on **L**, which eventually leads to continuation of riverside path.

❻ Turn **R** over footbridge back into Barnard Castle and go ahead into Thorngate. Turn **L** along Bridgegate. Where road crosses County Bridge, go straight on to follow path that rounds castle walls to entrance. After visiting castle, continue past Methodist church to start of Galgate.

❼ Turn **R** along Horse Market and continue to Market Cross. Carry on down The Bank then, at top of Thorngate, go **L** to Demesnes. Retrace earlier steps back to car park.

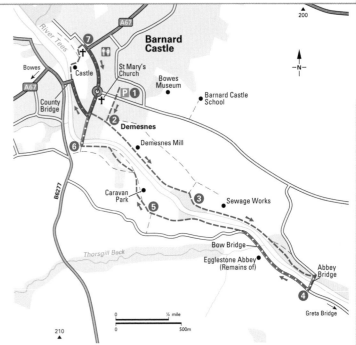

BALDERSDALE Wild Flowers And Moors

The spartan home of Hannah Hauxwell.

5.5 miles/8.8km 3hrs 15min **Ascent** 750ft/229m ⚠ **Difficulty** 2
Paths Tracks, field and moor paths and lanes, no stiles
Map OS Explorer OL31 North Pennines **Grid ref** NY 928187
Parking Car park by Balderhead dam

❶ Walk across Balderhead Dam causeway to south side of reservoir. Double back **L** on stony track descending past former youth hostel at Blackton Grange. Beyond this grass track leads down towards Blackton Reservoir where it meets Pennine Way track beyond gate. It's worth detouring **L** here to visit wetlands on northwest shores before returning to this point. Turn **R** along track and climb past Clove Lodge.
❷ Beyond this take tarmac lane **L**. On **L** you pass pastures of farms, while on **R** are barren slopes of Cotherstone Moor.
❸ Just beyond driveway of East Friar House, take narrow path climbing half **R** (southeast) towards rocks of Goldsborough (part of Bowes Loop Pennine Way alternative).
❹ By 1st of rocks, take **L** fork to climb to summit. Return to this position, then take narrow **R** fork path that descends northwards, back to road. Turn **R** along road and follow it down to Hury Reservoir.

❺ Just beyond Willoughby Hall, double back **L** along Northumbrian Water access track, then turn **R** off it along grassy causeway to north of reservoir. Path veers **L** above north shore and climbs above Blackton Dam to pair of gates. Through these, turn immediately **R** through another gate and head for further gate in northwest field corner.
❻ Path veers **R** alongside hawthorns, then turns **L** alongside more hawthorn trees. Past old barn, walls to **R** at first, then to **L**, guide route to footbridge across Blind Beck. Waymarking arrows now aid route-finding.
❼ Footpath now crosses 2 fields, parallel with reservoir's shoreline. In 3rd field, follow dry-stone wall half-**L** down towards Low Birk Hat, then pass in front of farmhouse to access road. House is private and it would be discourteous to pause too long here. Turn **R** on access road and climb out of valley, past Hannah's Meadow and High Birk Hat to higher road. Turn **L** then take next turning on **L**, tarmac lane leads to car.

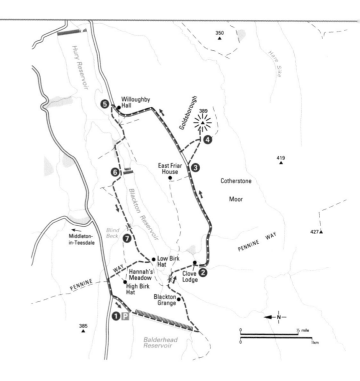

MARSDEN BAY Smugglers And The Light

Along the coast then inland to the hills.

5.5 miles/8.8km 2hrs **Ascent** 246ft/75m ⚠ **Difficulty** ① **Paths** Roads, tracks, field and coastal paths **Map** OS Explorer 316 Newcastle upon Tyne **Grid ref** NZ 412635 **Parking** Whitburn Coastal Park car park, signed off A183 – turn **R** after entrance and drive to southern end of road. If this National Trust car park is closed, use the municipal car park next to the Whitburn Lodge pub

❶ Leave car park at its southern end, following gravel track toward houses. Path goes past sign for Whitburn Point Nature Reserve. Follow track ahead through wall gap and turn **R**. Path bends **R**, **L** and **R** again to join road into houses. Go straight ahead to join main road.
❷ Cross road and turn **L**. Walk down road to windmill. Turn **R** to enter windmill grounds. Go up slope on path, then between houses. Bear **L**, then turn **R** to reach T-junction.
❸ Go straight ahead on path that goes to **R** of house No. 99. At another road turn **L**. Just after 1st bungalow on **R**, turn **R** along signed track. Follow track towards farm. Go through farmyard over 2 stiles and follow lane beyond, with hedge to **R**. Where it ends, turn **R** over stile.
❹ Follow path along field edge. Cross another stile, gradually ascending. Path bends **L** then **R**, still following field edge. Cross another 2 stiles. Path leads to tower of Cleadon Windmill.
❺ Go to **R** of windmill, following wall on **R**. Go **R**

through kissing gate, then bear slightly **R** (brick tower to **L**). Go parallel with wall on **R**. Cross track and go through wire mesh fence at right angles to wall. Follow path through scrubland to emerge by yellow post by golf course.
❻ Cross course, following yellow posts and looking out for golfers. Go over stone stile and turn **R** along signed footpath, following wall on **R**. Path eventually descends beside houses to road.
❼ Cross and take footpath almost opposite, to **R** of caravan site, heading towards sea. Carefully cross busy A183, then turn **R**, following sea edge. Marsden Rock is near by, and Marsden Grotto to **L** as you cross road. Follow coast as it bends **L** to Lizard Point. After visiting Souter Lighthouse, continue ahead on path slightly inland from coast, which returns you to car park.

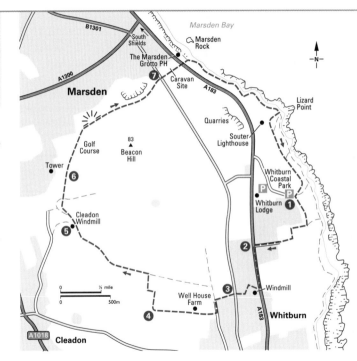

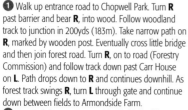

CHOPWELL Derwent Valley's Past
Steel making and Roman remains.

7 miles/11.3km 2hrs 30min **Ascent** 541ft/165m ▲ **Difficulty** 2
Paths Tracks, field paths and old railway line **Map** OS Explorer 307 Consett & Derwent Reservoir
Grid ref NZ122579 **Parking** Roadside parking in Chopwell; follow signs for 'Chopwell Park Car Park'.
Car park, itself, opens irregularly

❶ Walk up entrance road to Chopwell Park. Turn **R** past barrier and bear **R**, into wood. Follow woodland track to junction in 200yds (183m). Take narrow path on **R**, marked by wooden post. Eventually cross little bridge and then join forest road. Turn **R**, on to road (Forestry Commission) and follow track down past Carr House on **L**. Path drops down to **R** and continues downhill. As forest track swings **R**, turn **L** through gate and continue down between fields to Armondside Farm.

❷ Bear **R**; follow track to road in Blackhall Mill. Turn **L**, over bridge. Beyond, turn **L** by footpath sign and follow field-edge path **R** of hedge. Follow riverside path. At crossing path, turn **L**, uphill. At top go sharp **L**, following waymark signs. Go **L** of buildings, over stile and across field. Go over 2 stiles then **R**. Follow track uphill, passing Derwentcote Steel Furnace, to main road.

❸ Cross and take signed footpath almost opposite. Cross stile and, at crossing path, turn **R** to another stile. Follow path through woodland to former railway track.

Turn **R** and follow track, which crosses another track (barriers each side) and eventually rises to another barrier on to metalled lane.

❹ Turn **R**; descend into Ebchester. Bend **R** by community centre to main road. Cross; turn **R** in front of post office. Turn **L** at footpath sign beyond. Follow fence on **L**, bend **L** at end beside wall; follow footpath down to metalled lane. Turn **R** along lane to footbridge.

❺ Cross bridge. Footpath bends **R** before going ahead across field to stile. Follow green lane uphill, pass farmhouse and follow track through gates. Where main track bears **L**, go ahead. Go through gate and along field edge. Go though 2 gates to T-junction of tracks.

❻ Turn **L**, up track towards farm. 300yds (274m) after farm go **R**, through gate and walk across field to stile, hidden in hedge. Continue up field to another stile **R** of houses, and along narrow lane. At end, turn **R** along tarmac lane. At main road turn **R** and then **L**, following signs to 'Chopwell Park Car Park'.

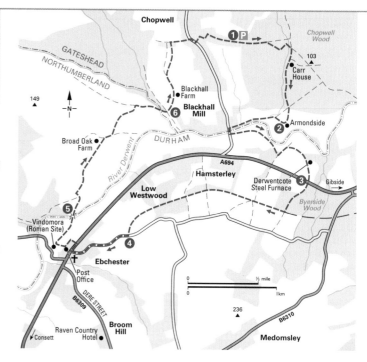

BERWICK-UPON-TWEED Town Walls

Exploring old Berwick.

6.5 miles/10.4km 2hrs 15min **Ascent** 98ft/30m ⚠ **Difficulty** ☐1

Paths Paved pathways and field paths; flood-meadows may be wet and muddy, particularly around high tide, 4 stiles **Map** OS Explorer 346 Berwick-upon-Tweed **Grid ref** NT 998529

Parking Below ramparts outside Scots Gate

NOTE Sheer, unguarded drop from outer edge of town walls and bastions, keep to marked pathways

❶ From old Town Hall, walk west along Marygate to Scots Gate. Just before it, turn **L** to gateway on **R**, climb on walls by Meg's Mount. Follow wall back over Scots Gate and past Cumberland Bastion.

❷ Brass Bastion, lies at northern corner of town. Soon path descends inside wall to meet The Parade by corner of church graveyard. Turn **R** past barracks to church.

❸ Return to walls and continue, passing Windmill Bastion and site of earlier Edward VI fort. Beyond King's Mount, walls rise above Tweed Estuary before turning upriver at Coxon's Tower, past elegant Georgian terraces and above old quay.

❹ Leave walls at Bridge End and cross Old Bridge. Turn **R** past war memorial, go beneath modern Royal Tweed Bridge and keep by river beyond, soon passing below Stephenson's railway viaduct.

❺ Continue upstream along (muddy) path. Where bank widens to meadow, pick up track on **L**, leading through kissing gates to open hide. Another gate leads on to next section of river bank. Eventually, beyond gate, contained path skirts water treatment plant. Turning **L** through 2nd gate, emerge on to tarmac track. Turn **R**.

❻ At bend 40yds (37m) on, bear **R** along field edge above steep river bank. Continue in next field but, towards far end, look for stepped path descending stream bank. Rising to stile, bear **R** to main road.

❼ Cross Tweed; drop **R** on to path, signed 'Berwick via Plantation'; cross 2 stiles to riverside pasture. Walk beside **L** boundary for 0.5 mile (800m). Cross head of stream, move from hedge, to meet the river below wooded bank. Over side bridge, bear **R** to stile and continue through trees beyond to path at top of bank.

❽ Go **R**, eventually dropping from wood by cottage, where riverside promenade leads to Berwick. Just beyond Royal Tweed Bridge, turn sharp **L**, climbing back beneath and beside town walls to Meg's Mount.

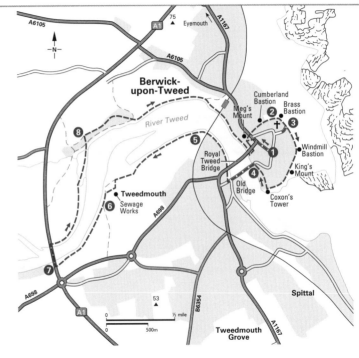

81

NORHAM The Tweed Valley

A delightful wander along the Tweed, returning past Norham's former railway station and ancient castle.

4.5 miles/7.2km 1hr 30min **Ascent** 205ft/62m ⚠ **Difficulty** 1
Paths Field and woodland paths, 4 stiles **Map** OS Explorer 339 Kelso & Coldstream
Grid ref NT 899473 **Parking** Roadside parking in Norham

❶ Leave village green by cross, heading along Pedwell Way to St Cuthbert's Church. In churchyard, walk along grassy path between graves to pass behind north side of church, to opening marking head of enclosed path down to Tweed. Follow river bank upstream, arriving at Ladykirk and Norham Bridge.

❷ Just beyond, go over stile on **L**, turn **R** and continue at field edge. Towards far end, approaching Bow Well Farm, look for stile which takes path down tree-clad bank and out to lane. Walk **R** and, at end, pass through gate, signed 'Twizell Bridge', to carry on across pasture in front of cottage, then through 2nd gate into wood. Undulating path continues above river.

❸ At path junction by footbridge, go **L** through broken gate. Bear **L** again little further on and climb to junction at top of wood. Now turn **R** to walk above Newbiggin Dean, passing beneath arch of railway viaduct. Shortly, at fork beyond stile, take **R** branch, signed 'East Biggin', which leads out on to lane.

❹ Turn **L**, climbing over hill to descend between piers of dismantled railway bridge. Just before here, to **L**, is former Norham Station, which closed in 1964. Buildings are now restored and house railway museum. Continue to end of lane.

❺ Turn **R**, but leave 250yds (229m) further on, through opening on **L**, signed as bridleway to Norham Castle. Keep ahead along field edge to bottom corner, where gated track continues beside brook through trees. Shortly, go **L** over bridge into field, and there turn **R**, following its edge out to lane. Turn **L** and walk past Norham Castle entrance, eventually returning to village.

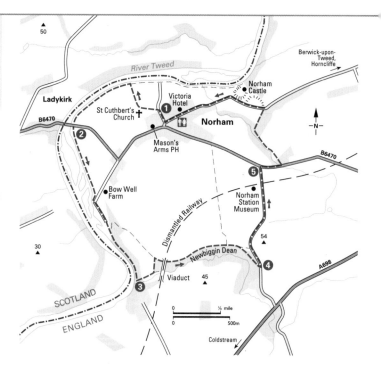

ETAL Estate Villages

Discover two very different estate villages.

6 miles/9.7km 2hrs **Ascent** 525ft/160m ⚠ **Difficulty** ☐1

Paths Lanes, tracks and field paths; 2 stiles on Walk 4

Map OS Explorer 339 Kelso & Coldstream **Grid ref** NT 925392

Parking Free car park by Etal Castle

❶ Walk through Etal to main road and turn **R** towards Ford, shortly leaving along lane on the **L-H** side to Letham Hill. At cottages, go **R** on track beside sawmill, signed 'Heatherslaw and Hay Farm', and keep on across fields.

❷ At bottom, by Shipton Dean, go through gate on **R** into strip of wood. Beyond, head down edge of fields to main road opposite Heatherslaw Station. Cross to lane opposite, following it over bridge and past Heatherslaw Mill.

❸ Keep going to Heatherslaw farm but, after **R-H** bend, leave through five-bar gate on **L**, signed 'Ford Bridge'. Pass shed and enter 2nd gate. Bear **R**, crossing to gate in far corner of field by river. Continue above Till to Ford Bridge, there following field edge away from river to gate leading to lane. Head back along it, crossing bridge to junction.

❹ To **R**, road winds up to Ford. Pass entrance to church and Ford Castle before turning **L** into village.

At bottom, opposite Lady Waterford Gallery, turn **R** to ascend to junction opposite Jubilee Cottage.

❺ Now go **L** but, where lane later bends sharply **R** beyond former stables, leave through gate on **L** into wood, signed 'Hay Farm'. Ignore obvious track ahead and bear **L** on path through trees to stream. Continue across bridge to emerge in field and follow perimeter to **L** above wood.

❻ Ignore corner gate and turn **R** up field edge to hill top. Here, pass **L** through gate and cross field to track in front of Hay Farm cottages.

❼ Walk as far as track on **R**, which leads past barns to junction. Turn **R** to enter gate 20yds (18m) on **L**, signed 'Heatherslaw and Letham Hill'. Follow field edge to power cable post, then go **R**, following boundary down and eventually passing wood to reach bottom corner. Drop through gate into trees to bridge over stream. Through gateway, turn **L** along field edge to return to Point **❷**. Retrace outward steps back to Etal.

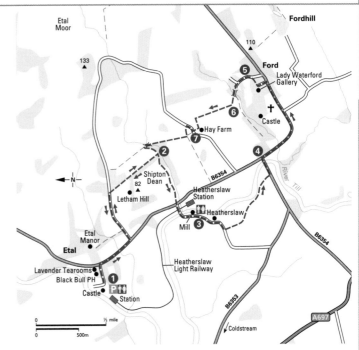

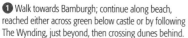

BAMBURGH Coat And Castle

Enjoy views to a castle and the Farne Islands.

8.5 miles/13.7km 3hrs 15min **Ascent** 450ft/137m ⚠ **Difficulty** ☐2
Paths Field paths, dunes and beach, 11 stiles **Map** OS Explorer 340 Holy Island & Bamburgh
Grid ref NU 183348 **Parking** Pay-and-display parking by Bamburgh Castle

① Walk towards Bamburgh; continue along beach, reached either across green below castle or by following The Wynding, just beyond, then crossing dunes behind.

② To **L**, sand soon gives way to Harkess Rocks. Carefully head round to lighthouse at Blackrocks Point (more easily negotiated to landward side). Continue below dunes, shortly regaining sandy beach to pass around Budle Point.

③ Before derelict pier, climb dunes towards World War II gun emplacement. Waymarked path behind rises on to golf course. Continue past markers to gate, leaving along track above caravan park. At bend, go through gate on **L** (blue 'Coast Path' marker) and continue along field edge to cottages at Newtown.

④ Beyond, follow field boundary on **L** to regain golf course through kissing gate at top field corner. Bear **R** to pass **L** of look-out; continue on grass track to main road.

⑤ Turn **L** and walk down Galliheugh Bank to bend and turn off to Dukesfield. Approaching lane's end, go **L** over stile and walk past house, crossing 2 stiles in field's far corner. Continue by hedge to road. Cross to follow green lane opposite and just after cottage, reach stile on **L**. Make for West Burton farm, turn **R** through farmyard to lane, then go **L**.

⑥ Beyond bend and over stile on **L**, signed 'New Shorestone', bear half **R** across field. Emerging on to lane, cross stile opposite and continue in same direction to Ingram Lane.

⑦ 300yds (274m) to **L**, gated track on **R** leads away, then around to **L** towards Fowberry. Meeting narrow lane, go **L** to farm, then turn **R** before entrance on to green track. In next field, follow **L** perimeter around corner to metal gate. Through that, keep beside **R-H** wall to double gate, there turning **R** across final field to Greenhill. Keep ahead to main road.

⑧ Continue across to beach and head north to Bamburgh. Approaching castle, turn inland, over dunes, where cattle fence can be crossed by one of several gates or stiles. Work your way through to regain road by car park.

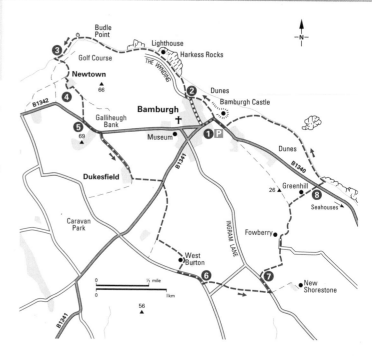

KIRKNEWTON Ancient Yeavering Bell

Views of the Cheviot Hills and the sea are the reward for climbing to this hilltop fort.

5 miles/8km 2hrs 15min **Ascent** 1,115ft/340m ⚠ **Difficulty** ③
Paths Tracks, field paths and moorland, steep ascent and descent
Map OS Explorer OL16 The Cheviot Hills **Grid ref** NT 914302
Parking In Kirknewton village, in wide area of road beyond school and church, off B6351

❶ From car, walk towards village centre, then turn **L**. Just before gate, bend **R** along lane, following 'Hillforts Trail' sign. Metalled lane bends **R** again and becomes grassy track. Go through metal gate and straight on at next waymarker. Go through 2 more metal gates and gateway. At next marker post bear **R**, signed 'Permissive Path' and cross stream and ladder stile.

❷ Turn **L** after stile, then cross another stile. Bear half **R** across field to hand gate in crossing wall. Go through gate, and bear **R** to reach waymarked post beside track. This is part of St Cuthbert's Way.

❸ Turn **L** along track and follow it through wooden waymarked gate, past farmhouse and over cattle grid. Just before next cattle grid, turn **R** off track, following 'St Cuthbert's Way' sign. Bend **L** through gate and continue along grassy track uphill to ladder stile in wall **L**.

❹ Cross stile and turn **R** to follow footpath uphill. At low-level signpost, turn **L**, signed 'Yeavering Bell'. Follow waymarks down into valley, across stream, then uphill. Path eventually passes through fort wall. Bend **R** to

summit of Yeavering Bell.

❺ After enjoying view, go down to valley between 2 peaks. Bear **R** and head downhill, on opposite side of hill to that which you came up. Go through wall and follow waymark beyond. Path is waymarked all way down steep hill to stile.

❻ Cross stile, then ladder stile on **R** on to track. Follow track past marker post and, just after it, bend **L** towards another track, which leads towards farm buildings in valley bottom. Go over ladder stile by buildings and turn **R** along track. Go through metal gate and past cottages to reach road. Site of Ad Gefrin palace can be visited from access path here.

❼ Turn **L** along road and follow it back to Kirknewton. At 'Yetholm' sign at entrance to the village go ahead, through gate, then turn **R** back to car parking area.

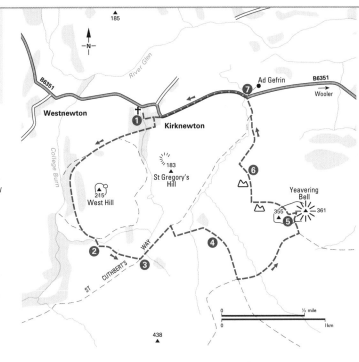

CHILLINGHAM Wild Cattle

A superb walk that encircles a haunted castle and the home of the only wild cattle left in Britain.

6 miles/9.7km 3hrs **Ascent** 754ft/230m ⚠ **Difficulty** 2
Paths Hill track, surfaced road
Map OS Explorer 340 Holy Island & Bamburgh **Grid ref** NU 071248
Parking Forest car park at Hepburn Wood

❶ Leave car park, turn **R** and go uphill for 0.5 mile (800m) and round bend to National Trust notice indicating Ros Castle. Follow track to gate in wall **L** and go through gate into Chillingham Wood. Turn **R**, then **L** and follow marker posts on to broader track after 100yds (91m). This leads uphill, then across level stretch to fence. On **L** is view over Chillingham Park, where you might see wild cattle.

❷ Turn **R** at fence and go uphill as indicated by signpost to Chillingham. At wall, turn **L** and follow track between wall and fence to picnic table. Continue to next forest, and walk between wall and forest for 250yds (229m) to next signpost to Chillingham.

❸ Turn **L** and descend through forest, following marker posts. When small track reaches junction with track signed 'Forest Walk', turn **R** and continue to signpost. Take Chillingham direction, through 2 tall kissing gates to picnic area with 2 tables.

❹ Continue along track to forest road and turn **R** on to this, which becomes metalled lower down. Sign points **L** over small bridge, back into woods, following red markers. Track rises to gate in deer fence, then levels off to run parallel with wall. Continue beyond picnic tables to gate and turn **R**. Keep **R** at next junction, down hill. Keep **R** again to descend to road in front of Garden Cottage.

❺ Turn **L** and follow road past Church of St Peter, on **L**, then past gate leading to Chillingham Castle. Cross Hollow Burn either by ford or footbridge and continue to T-junction with main road. Turn **L** and follow road, passing main castle gate after 550yds (500m).

❻ At next fork in road, take **L** fork and go uphill to crossroads. Road is not busy with traffic and has good grass verges for walking. Turn **L** on road to Hepburn Farm. Follow this, past farm buildings, and continue to Hepburn Wood car park.

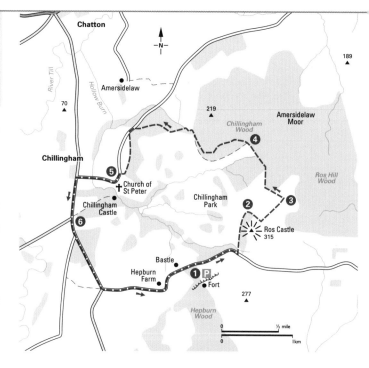

BREAMISH VALLEY Burned Hamlets

The remains of an ancient settlement.

7.5 miles/12.1km 4hrs (5hrs if following detours) **Ascent** 1,312ft/400m ⚠ **Difficulty** ③
Paths Part metalled road, part hill tracks, all stiles alongside gates
Map OS Explorer OL16 The Cheviot Hills **Grid ref** NT 976162
Parking Roadside parking at Hartside

❶ From Hartside, take metalled road signposted to Alnhammoor, over cattle grid, then turn sharp **R** and downhill. At bottom of hill, road turns **L** and leads to wooden bridge. Cross bridge and continue steadily uphill, past farm and across 3 more cattle grids. Impressive river valley is **L**.

❷ Near top of 1st rise, another track joins main roadway from **L**. You are now on side of Meggrim's Knowe. Trackless detour over hill to **R** and down to shoulder on other side will bring you, in 0.25 mile (400m) to remains of the Celtic settlement.) Continue on metalled road, which follows contour and gives spectacular views into Breamish valley. Road swings **L**, descends gently to river, then turns **L** again through narrow gorge to Low Bleakhope farm. Beyond, valley opens out to High Bleakhope. Continue past this and 2 small woods beyond, to gate.

❸ Follow signposted public bridleway to **R**, steeply uphill to gate and stile. Go through gate and continue less steeply, following guide posts for 550 yards (500m) to next gate, through this and across to 3rd gate 220 yards (200m) further on. Beyond, 3 tracks diverge. Take middle track across open moorland, with views **L** toward Cheviot and Hedgehope Hill, Northumberland's highest peaks. Continue past walk's highest point, Rig Cairn, then downhill to fence across saddle.

❹ Go through gate and down to side of forest, passing through another gate on way. Linhope Spout can be reached by following lower track **L** along forest edge, through kissing gate and downhill for 0.25 mile (400m). Back on main route, follow rubble track to **R** to reach Linhope hamlet after 0.25 mile (400m).

❺ Metalled road leads across bridge and uphill for 220yds (201m), to where broad track on **L** leads into field alongside forest. To visit Grieve's Ash, go on to track, then follow forest edge steeply uphill for 110yds (100m). Main road leads back to your car.

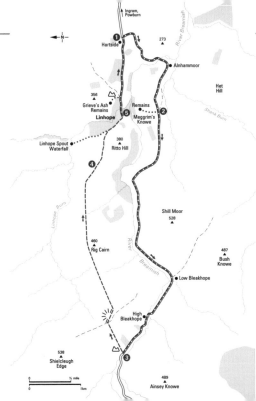

ALWINTON The Gorge of the River Coquet
A demanding but spectacular walk.

4.5 miles/7.2km 3hrs **Ascent** 590ft/180m 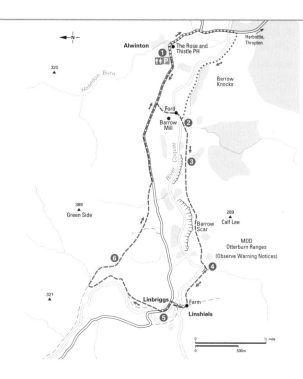 **Difficulty** 3

Paths Mostly hill footpaths, some narrow with severe drops on one side. River forded at one point, 8 stiles **Map** OS Explorer OL16 The Cheviot Hills **Grid ref** NT 919063

Parking Car park at Alwinton **NOTE** This walk requires you to ford the River Coquet near Barrow Mill. If the water level is too high, use the alternative start from Alwinton

1 Turn **R** from car park; follow road for 700yds (640m) to gate **L** leading to Barrow Mill. Go through gate and down to farm. Go through gate and cross field to gate to river bank. Ford river. After rain, your feet will get wet. If the water is too high, return to Alwinton and walk along main road to bridge over Coquet. A few yards beyond, look for stile **R** and follow path across meadows to ruin at Barrow.

2 Enter field and follow fence to **R** to gate. Go through this or over stile 20yds (18m) **L** and continue to derelict farm. Follow track up hill to **R-H** corner of conifer forest.

3 50yds (46m) before reaching signpost marking edge of military firing range, follow less well-defined track across heather-covered hillside **R** rising slightly, to reach wire fence. Follow this over top of Barrow Scar, with fence **R**. At 2nd fence, follow this to stile. Cross stile and go down to obvious loop in river. In late summer, bracken here may be deep and track obscured.

4 At river bend, cross stile, then another after another 100yds (91m). Cross field and stile into farmyard at Linshiels. Go through farmyard, across 2 bridges and join road. Turn **L** and follow road until just past farm buildings, to signpost pointing to Shillmoor.

5 Go up hillside, cross stile and follow track overlooking gorge and waterfalls. For short distance, slopes below are quite precipitous and care is needed, though track is good. Continue alongside river, descending eventually to sheep pens and ford. Continue ahead, now ascending larger path to intersect bridleway. Turn **R** and double back, crossing stream and passing through gates before ascending hillside on broad sweeping path.

6 At top of slope continue across level ground, then descend to stile. Cross this and follow track, over another stile and down to road. Follow road for 1 mile (1.6km) back to Alwinton.

CRASTER A Ruined Castle

The castle that inspired artist J M W Turner.

5 miles/8km 1hr 45min **Ascent** 275ft/84m ▲ **Difficulty** ⊡
Paths Generally good tracks, some field paths tussocky, 1 stile
Map OS Explorer 332 Alnwick & Amble **Grid ref** NU 256198
Parking Pay-and-display behind Craster tourist information centre

❶ From car park, turn **R** towards village. Immediately before harbour, go **L** into Dunstanburgh Road, signed 'Castle', and continue through gate at end above rocky shore heading towards Dunstanburgh Castle.

❷ After 2 more gates, to visit castle keep to main track, which winds around to its entrance. Otherwise, bear **L** on less-distinct path through shallow gorge on landward side. Continuing below castle, pass ruins of Lilburn Tower, perched dramatically atop rocky spur outcrop.

❸ Beyond, passing above bouldery beach, glance back to cliffs protecting Dunstanburgh Castle's northern side, which, in early summer, echo to screams of innumerable seabirds, squabbling for nesting sites.

❹ Through kissing gate at edge of golf course, bear **R** to remain above shore, where dramatic folding of rocks is evident. Ahead stretches sandy expanse of Embleton Bay and, if tide permits, continue along beach.

❺ Shortly, look for prominent break in dunes, through which path leads across golf course to meet lane.

Follow it up to Dunstan Steads, turning **L** immediately before on to drive, signed 'Craster'. Where it bends behind buildings, bear **L** across open area to gate and continue over open fields on farm track.

❻ After 1 mile (1.6km), at Dunstan Square, pass through 2 successive gates by barn, then turn **L** through 3rd gate, signed 'Craster'. Walk down field edge, through another gate at bottom, then on along track rising through break in cliffs ahead, The Heughs. Keep going across top to field corner and turn through gate on **R**.

❼ Walk away, initially beside **L-H** boundary, but after 150yds (137m), by gate, bear **R** to follow line of ridge higher up. Eventually meeting corner of wall, continue ahead beside it. Shortly after crossing track, go on over stile, after which path becomes more enclosed. Approaching village, path turns abruptly **L** behind house and emerges on to street. Follow it down to main lane and turn **R**, back to car park.

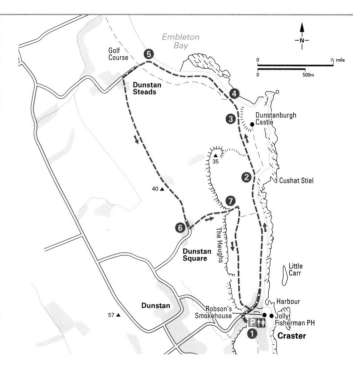

OTTERBURN Medieval And Modern Battlefields

Skirt a medieval battlefield and a training ground for modern warriors.

4.5 miles/7.2km 2hrs **Ascent** 300ft/91m ⚠ **Difficulty** 1
Paths Bridleway, moorland track and metalled road
Map OS Explorer OL42 Kielder Water & Forest **Grid ref** NY 889929
Parking Roadside car park at eastern end of Otterburn village

❶ From car park, walk through Otterburn. 100yds (91m) after passing Church of St John the Evangelist, turn **R** on to road to Otterburn Hall. At top of incline, go on to public bridleway on **L**, past farm buildings and into field. Follow bridleway alongside wall and through gate into next field. Continue, now with wall, which gives way to wire fence, on **R**.

❷ Go through next gate and, maintaining direction, cross field to gate through opposite wall. Go through gate and across marshy ground past plantation, now mostly cut down, to junction with metalled road. Follow this to **R**, across cattle grid and around bend to **L**, up gentle incline.

❸ 100yds (91m) after bend, follow grassy track across hillside to **R**, past sheep pen. This leads to gate, beyond which is military warning notice. Go through gate and continue across moorland, gently downhill. Ground is boggy and track indefinite in places, but it leads to better track, which follows fence on **R** to join metalled road at Hopefoot farm.

❹ Follow road to **R**, crossing bridge over stream, then through woods, to join old main access road to army camp at Hopefoot Cottages. Turn **R** and follow road past Doe Crag cottages and across bridge to entrance to Otterburn Hall. Go through gate opposite this on to footpath, signposted to Otterburn and leading across field.

❺ Follow track, passing sports centre on **R**. At bend in wire fence, track forks. Follow **L** fork downhill, across 2 small footbridges, through kissing gate and along river bank. Track may be muddy and overgrown at times. After crossing stile, track brings you into Otterburn, just opposite Percy Arms. Turn **L** and return to car park.

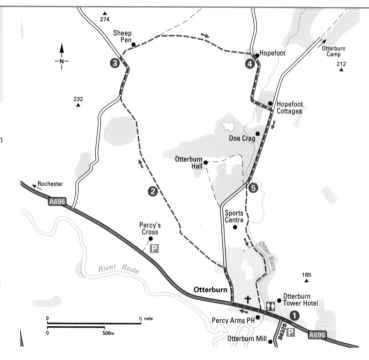

SIMONSIDE HILLS Ancient Spirit

A hill that had spiritual significance to early settlers and now popular with rock climbers.

5.5 miles/8.8km 3hrs **Ascent** 820ft/250m ⚠ **Difficulty** ③
Paths Generally good tracks, but steep and muddy in places
Map OS Explorer OL42 Kielder Water & Forest **Grid ref** NZ 037997
Parking Large car park at forest picnic area

❶ From notice board in picnic area, go through gate on to broad forest road. Follow this gently uphill, swinging **R** round long hairpin bend, then back **L** at top of hill. When road splits, take **R-H** fork, past communications mast and go gently downhill. At next junction, take **L-H** fork and follow road past sign indicating detour to Little Church Rock.
❷ At marker post, where narrow track leads to **L**, ignore this and continue along broad track, now grassy. After passing huge, heavily overgrown boulder, continue to small cairn which marks start of subsidiary track on **L**. Follow track uphill through forest and out on to heather-covered hillside. You see Simonside's crags 0.5 mile (800m) away **L**.
❸ Continue up narrow track to join broader one at edge of upper forest and follow this **L** for 275yds (251m) to corner of trees. A rough track, sometimes muddy in places, picks its way through boulders up

hillside. Follow this, keeping crags on **L-H** side, on to plateau and walk on paved route along top of crags to large summit cairn, which is probably burial mound.
❹ Away from summit, track splits into 2. Follow **R** fork, still paved across boggy ground for 0.3 mile (530m). Climb short rise keeping wonderfully wind-sculpted Old Stell Crag to **L** and move round on to summit and another large cairn.
❺ Take narrow path down to join lower track. This joins paved route again in 0.5 mile (800m), by cairn on Dove Crag. Now descend rocky staircase and cross ladder stile, keeping direction along broad ridge path uphill to The Beacon cairn. Continue downhill for 0.5 mile (800m) to join road at Lordenshaws car park.
❻ Turn **L** and follow road for 1 mile (1.6km) to reach forest picnic area at start.

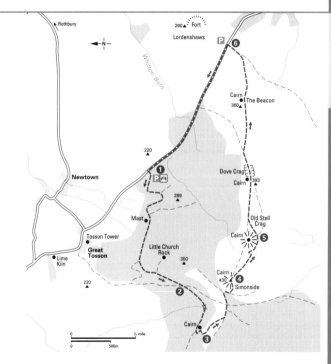

ELSDON Reiver Country

A walk in the hills and valleys.

4 miles/6.4km 1hr 45min **Ascent** 623ft/190 ⚠ **Difficulty** ②

Paths Field paths and tracks

Map OS Explorer OL42 Kielder Water & Forest **Grid ref** NY 937932

Parking Car park in Elsdon, by bridge on Rothbury road

❶ From car park, pass village hall and toilets on **R**. Go through gateway and climb up lane past Mote Hills. Pass house and cross gravel to gate. Cross small field and go through next gate, then head half **R** to go through gate near some trees. Follow path up sunken lane, then along field edge to gate.

❷ Go through gate and turn **L** over cattle grid. Follow metalled lane through farm buildings and down to cottages. Opposite them, turn **R** in front of barn, cross stream and go through gate.

❸ Cross field with bank on **L** and, at top of rise, bear **L** across bank, making for gate in crossing wire fence. After gate, bear half **L** crossing ditches to **L-H** end of crossing wall.

❹ Turn **R** and follow wall downhill. Go through gateway in crossing wall, and continue to follow wall on **L** to reach waymarked post. Turn **R**, cross small bridge, then go uphill to gate and ladder stile on **L**, before building. This signposted permissive route leaves right of way. Cross stile to join road and turn **L**. Cross cattle grid, then bridge to reach 2nd cattle grid.

❺ Cross grid, then immediately turn **R**, signed 'East Todholes'. Cross stream and go through gate, then cross 2nd stream. Follow wall on **L** to ladder stile by pine trees. After stile, bear half **L** to go round the **R-H** side of East Todholes farm and cross stile on to lane.

❻ Follow lane past next farm and up hill to join road. Turn **R** and, in short distance, cross stile over fence **R**. Head half **L**, down field to reach old wall. Follow this downhill towards Elsdon, bending **R**, then **L** at fence to cross stile. After another stile, bear **R** to footbridge, then **L** to another. Path brings you to larger footbridge near village.

❼ Cross footbridge, then turn **R** to stile beside gate. Go up track between houses to road to green. Bear **R**, along edge of green, cross bridge and go back to village hall at start.

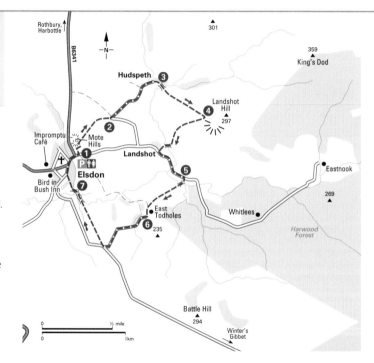

DRURIDGE BAY A Beachy Nature Reserve

A nature reserve, country park and beach.

5.5 miles/8.8km 1hr 45min **Ascent** Negligible **⚠ Difficulty** 1
Paths Paths and tracks, with good walk on beach, no stiles
Map OS Explorers 325 Morpeth & Blyth; 332 Alnwick & Amble **Grid ref** NU 282024 (on Explorer 332)
Parking Car park at Hauxley Nature Reserve
NOTE Check tides; complete coastal section not always passable at high water

❶ Waymarked footpath beside car park entrance winds between nature reserve and caravan site towards coast. Through gate at bottom, turn **R** on track, which shortly passes 2 gates that give access to bird hides overlooking lake.

❷ Leaving reserve, continue little further along tarmac track to informal parking area on **L**, where there is easy access on to beach. Now, follow shore past Togston Links, across stream and on below Hadston Links.

❸ After 1.25 miles (2km), wooden steps take path off sands on to dunes. Cross tarmac track and continue over marshy area into pinewood. Beyond trees, emerge by car park and walk across to Druridge Bay Country Park visitor centre (café and toilets).

❹ Footway **L** winds around Ladyburn Lake, soon passing boat launching area. Keep to lower path, which soon leads to stepping-stones across upper neck of lake. If you would rather not cross here, continue around upper edge of wooded nature sanctuary above water to footbridge higher up. Cross bridge, turn immediately **R**, through gate into nature sanctuary. Follow river bank back though another gate to reach far side of stepping-stones.

❺ Path winds through trees to emerge beside lushly vegetated shoreline where swans feed. After crossing bridge over lake's outflow, return to visitor centre.

❻ Retrace steps to beach and turn back towards Hauxley, but at point where you originally dropped on to sands, remain on shore towards Bondi Carrs. Seaweed can make the rocks slippery, so be careful clambering over them as you round point, where Coquet Island comes into view. Not far beyond, after passing look-out post and approaching large rocks (storm defence), leave across dunes, retracing outward path short distance back to start.

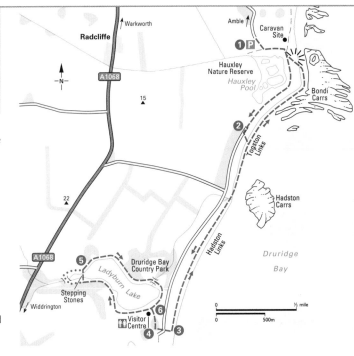

MORPETH Along The River Wansbeck

A fine woodland valley walk.

8.5 miles/13.7km 2hrs 45min **Ascent** 420ft/128m ⚠ **Difficulty** ☐1☐
Paths Woodland paths (muddy after rain) and field paths, 8 stiles
Map OS Explorer 325 Morpeth & Blyth **Grid ref** NZ 198859
Parking Car parks within town

❶ From Town Hall, walk east along Bridge Street to end, continuing to **L** along main road towards Pegswood. After Old Red Bull Inn, take enclosed path on **R** that later rejoins main road. Cross to footpath rising through woodland opposite, signed 'Whorral Bank and Cottingwood Common'. Bear **R** at fork, past residential home, then go **R** at junction to again meet main road.
❷ On far side, path, signed 'Bothal', descends into lushly wooded valley through which flows River Wansbeck. There follows delightful, undulating walk for 2.25 miles (3.6km), ending by sawmill. Walk to lane beyond, and turn **R** across river.
❸ After climbing from valley, lane continues above wood. Where it later bends sharply **L** at Shadfen Cottage, go ahead across stile into field corner, and carry on at edge of fields beside **R-H** boundary. Eventually, way passes **R** of deep excavation, once opencast coal mine, before falling towards stile into woodland. Drop through trees to bridge over stream.

❹ Re-emerging into open fields above far bank, follow path ahead between cultivation to gain tarmac track past Parkhouse Banks. After 120yds (110m), immediately beyond drive, turn through gap in **R-H** hedge, signed 'Whorral Bank', and walk beside field edge. At corner, slip **R** through gap and carry on along track past cottage and through fields to railway bridge.
❺ Keep over field beyond to stile, there dropping across rough pasture back into wood. Soon joined by track, continue to junction by river and turn **L** above bank. Emerging from trees, bear **L** along field path past cottage, ongoing track returning to river.
❻ Over bridge, street leads past ambulance station into town. Go ahead to St George's Church and then turn **L** over Telford Bridge to Castle Square. Cross into Carlisle Park and, beyond flowerbeds, bear **R** following main drive to riverside promenade. Walk upstream past Elliott Bridge to top of park and turn **R** over Oldgate Bridge to return to start.

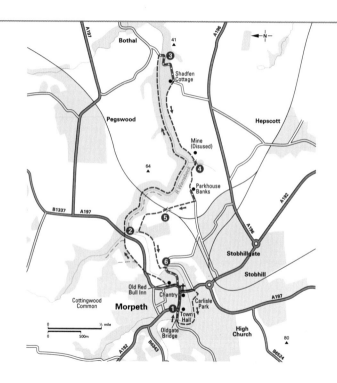

LANEHEAD A Once-Lawless Landscape
Hills and valleys with an interesting village.

7.5 miles/12.1km 3hrs **Ascent** 1,083ft/330m ⚠ **Difficulty** 2
Paths Burnside, moorland paths and tracks – some wet areas
Map OS Explorer OL42 Kielder Water & Forest **Grid ref** NY 793858
Parking Beside Tarset Village Hall in Lanehead, on Greenhaugh road

1 At staggered crossroads Lanehead turn **R**, signed 'Donkleywood'. At Redmire cottages turn **R** through gate, and cross yard to leave by 2 more gates. Cross field, passing through gap to reach hand gate. Bear **L**, descending to kissing gate by river. Follow river bank **R**, through gates before rising to final gate and dropping to bridge. Cross Tarset Burn and follow path down ramp to join farm track. Turn **L** along this to farmyard.

2 Go though farmyard and ascend track on far side. As it bears **L**, go ahead past waymarker and down to cross stream. Pass waymarked post and go through gateway. Bend **R** and go through hand gate. Turn **L** along fence, then, at stile, bear half **R** across open moor towards woods and church. Keep **L** of ruined wall, aiming for dilapidated shed and wall descending to bridge over burn.

3 Cross stream. Veer **L** on opposite bank to locate gate at side of garden. Go through this and follow track beside churchyard to road. Turn **R** and at T-junction turn **L**. Follow lane past Redheugh farm and 'Forestry Commission Sidwood' sign to Sidwood Picnic Area, near white-painted buildings.

4 Follow path into wood on **L**, but soon look for **R** turn, crossing burn and continuing up hill. Cross forest track and continue up hill through clear fell. Maintain direction as route levels, now with ditch **R**. On descending, forest gives way to moorland **L** and you reach gate. Continue down through enclosure, crossing burn then rising to crossing track. Turn **L** and follow down to cross burn with care at Slaty Ford.

5 Continue on prominent enclosed track to gate. Beyond, follow minor road for 1 mile (1.6km) along flank of North Tyne valley passing through gate after 0.5 mile (800m) to junction. Keep ahead, over cattle grid and down to bridge over Tarset Burn. Continue on lane as it ascends bank to main road. Turn **L** to return to car.

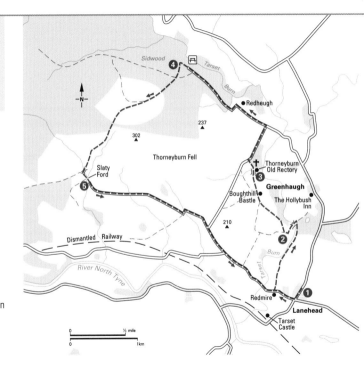

CORBRIDGE Romans And Countryside

Discover Corbridge, Catherine Cookson's home and a rich history.

6 miles/9.7km 3hrs 30min **Ascent** 525ft/160m ⚠ **Difficulty** 2

Paths Village streets, riverside and farm paths and lanes, 8 stiles

Map OS Explorer OL43 Hadrian's Wall **Grid ref** NY 992642

Parking On town centre streets, or in free long stay car park over bridge

❶ From Low Hall Pele head west down Main Street before turning **R** up Princes Street. At town hall turn **L** along Hill Street, then, just before church, turn **L** up narrow street to pass Vicar's Pele. Turn **R** at Market Place and head north up Watling Street, then Stagshaw Road, which is staggered **L** beyond Wheatsheaf Inn.

❷ Go **L** along Trinity Terrace then **L** again along footpath, signed 'West Green'. This leads past Catherine Cookson's old house, Town Barns, to Georgian house of Orchard Vale. Turn **R** then **L** along lane to river.

❸ Turn Lalong Carelgate, then follow riverside path to town bridge. Cross bridge, then follow south banks of Tyne on unsurfaced track passing cricket ground at Tynedale Park before mounting grassy embankment parallel to river.

❹ Turn **R** up steps, go over ladder stile, then cross railway tracks (with care). Another stile and more steps lead path through wood and across field to meet A695 where you turn **R** – footpath on nearside.

❺ Beyond cottages, turn **L** up country lane, which zig-zags up Prospect Hill. After 1st bend leave lane for southbound path that climbs fields. Just short of woods path meets track; turn **R** for few paces to rejoin lane. Follow this and reach crossroads at hill top. Turn **R**.

❻ Pass Temperley Grange and West farms and leave road for path on **R** that follows first the **R-H** side, then **L-H** side of dry-stone wall across high fields and down to Snokoehill Plantations.

❼ Go through gate to enter wood, then turn **L** along track running along top edge. Track doubles back **R**, soon to follow bottom edge of woods.

❽ Turn **R** beyond gate above High Town farm and follow track, which becomes tarred beyond West Fell.

❾ Beyond Roecliff Lodge path on **L** crosses field to reach A695 road. Across other side of road path enters copse, The Scrogs, before joining B6529 by Corbridge Railway Station. Follow this over bridge and back into Corbridge.

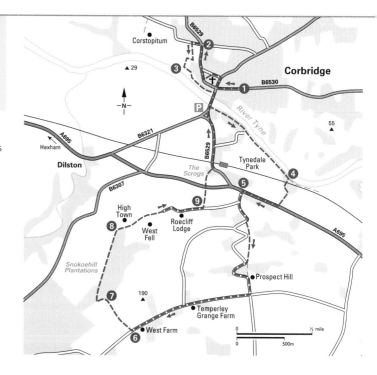

HEXHAM An Historic Town
A walk round the abbey and market town.

3.75 miles/6km 2hrs **Ascent** 590ft/180m ⚠ **Difficulty** 1
Paths Town streets, lanes and woodland paths, 4 stiles
Map OS Explorer OL43 Hadrian's Wall **Grid ref** NY 939641
Parking Pay-and-display car park, next to supermarket

1 From car park (not supermarket end) take exit between TIC and café to follow narrow street past Old Gaol. Go under arches of Moot Hall and enter Market Place. Take tour of The Sele, park grounds surrounding Hexham Abbey, before aiming roughly southwest across them to Queen Hall on Beaumont Street.
2 Turn **R** to Benson's Monument, then continue ahead on unnamed street. After taking 1st turning **R**, ignore Elvaston Road on **L**, but go ahead on tarred lane that leads to foot of Cowgarth Dene.
3 At bridge, turn off into woodland where now unsurfaced track crosses footbridge and climbs out to little park at edge of housing estate. Follow woodland edge, then track past water treatment works and new houses.
4 Turn **L** through gate to reach estate proper into Wydon Water car park. Turn **R** along grassy ride, dipping **L** through hedgerow after 110yds (100m) to round head of reservoir. At lane, turn **L**, following it up hill, where it becomes unsurfaced, past house.

5 Emerging on road, turn **L** then, at Intake farm, turn **R** along path that leads into thick woodland of Wydon Burn's upper reaches. Narrow path continues through woods to reach lane at Causey Hill; turn **L** past campsite to junction with road known as The Yarridge. Modern building here is part of Hexham Racecourse.
6 Turn **L** along road and go ahead at crossroads.
7 Beyond Black House stile **L** marks start of downhill, cross-field path into Hexham. Beyond step stile path veers **R** to round gorse bushes before resuming its course alongside **L** field edge.
8 Just before reaching whitewashed cottage, cross stile on **L** and follow road into town. Turn **L** along shopping street at bottom, then **R** along St Mary's Chare, back to Market Place.

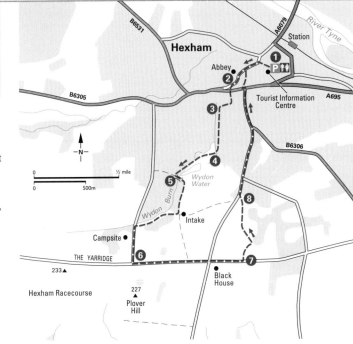

CRAG LOUGH Along The Emperor's Wall

A moorland walk along Hadrian's Wall.

8 miles/12.9km 4hrs **Ascent** 885ft/270m ⚠ **Difficulty** ③
Paths Mainly well walked National Trails, 16 stiles
Map OS Explorer OL43 Hadrian's Wall **Grid ref** NY 750677
Parking Steel Rigg (pay) car park **NOTE** Please don't damage wall by walking on it

❶ From car park descend to grassy depression beneath Peel Crags. Path arcs **L** and climbs back to ridge in series of steps before following cliff tops past Turret 39a and Milecastle 39.

❷ After another dip, climb to Highshield Crags, which overlook Crag Lough. Beyond lake footpath climbs past Hotbank farm.

❸ At the dip, Rapishaw Gap, turn **L** over ladder stile and follow faint waymarked Pennine Way route across undulating moorland. 1st stile lies in far **R** corner of large rushy enclosure. Clear cart track develops beyond dyke and climbs to ridge on Ridley Common; turn half **L** to descend grassy ramp.

❹ Path arcs **R** to cross fenced cart track at Cragend. Grassy track zig-zags to moorland depression with Greenlee Lough **L**. At bottom, ground can be marshy and path indistinct in places. Waymark points sharp **R** but the loses itself on bank above. Head north, keeping farmhouse, East Stonefolds, at ten to the hour.

Next stile lies in kink in cross wall.

❺ Beyond, turn half **L** to traverse a field. Cross ladder stile and turn **L** along farm track, which passes through East Stonefolds. Track ends at West Stonefolds. Walk through farmyard, heeding plea from residents not to intrude too much on their privacy.

❻ Past house continue, with wall **L**, along grassy ride, and go over step stile to reach signposted junction. Go ahead on permissive path (' Greenlee Lough Birdhide'). Path follows fence to lake. Ignore (to hide), and continue alongside fence.

❼ Cross next stile and wetlands north of lake on duckboard path, which soon swings **R** to gate. Beyond, continue on path, climbing northwest, guided by waymarker posts to farm track by clearfelled stumps of Greenlee Plantation.

❽ Turn **L** along track; follow it past Gibbs Hill farm. Past farmhouse tarmac lane leads back towards wall. Turn **L** at T-junction to return to car.

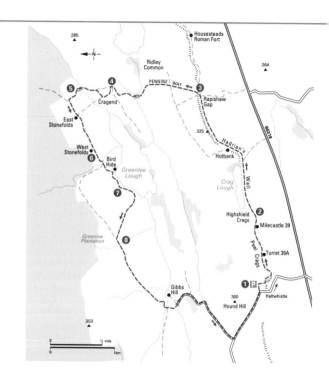

ALLEN BANKS Gorgeous Grounds

A walk through a wooded gorge.

5 miles/8km 2hrs 45min **Ascent** 420ft/128m ⚠ **Difficulty** ②
Paths Well-signposted woodland paths, 7 stiles
Map OS Explorer OL43 Hadrian's Wall **Grid ref** NY 798640
Parking National Trust pay-and-display car park

❶ Follow riverside path from back of car park and stay with lower **L** fork where path divides. Stay on Allen's west banks rather than crossing suspension bridge. Beyond, path tucks beneath Raven Crag. River bends to **R** and you soon enter nature reserve at Briarwod Banks. Here the ancient woodland has seen continuous growth dating back to the end of the last ice age. With broadleaved trees like sessile oak, wych elm, ash, birch, rowan and alder flourishing, this is a haven for wildlife, and more than 60 species of birds have been recorded in the valley.

❷ On Briarwood Banks path uses footbridge across Kingswood Burn, then turn **L** across new bridge over Allen to Plankey Mill.

❸ Turn **R** along field edge path close to river and cross either of 2 step stiles into woodland. If you choose riverside stile steps lead you back to main track. You are now following green waymarks of Staward Pele path which stays close to river, though

it's often high above banks. Just beyond footbridge path divides. Take **R** fork – the **L** is your downhill return route.

❹ On reaching top eastern edge of woods path turns **L** where it first passes gatehouse of Staward Pele, then ruins of fortified farm.

❺ Beyond pele track descends, steeply, sometimes in steps back to previously mentioned footbridge. Retrace steps to Plankey Mill.

❻ At tarred lane by mill, turn **R**, go uphill along it, then, at sharp bend, turn off on enclosed footpath. This leads to footpath that follows field edge alongside river's east bank.

❼ Turn **L** over suspension bridge opposite Morralee Wood turn off, then turn **R** along outward footpath back to car park.

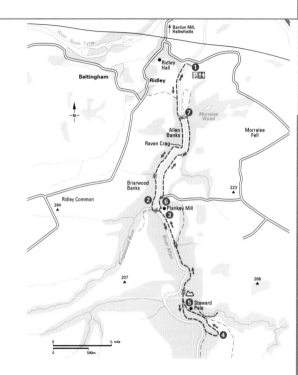

ALLENDALE TOWN Shining Water

Exploring an attractive river valley.

3.75 miles/6km 2hrs 15min **Ascent** 590ft.180m ⚠ **Difficulty** ☐ 1

Paths Good river paths and faint field paths, 19 stiles

Map OS Explorer OL43 Hadrian's Wall **Grid ref** NY 838558

Parking Ample parking in village centre

❶ From Market Place take Whitfield road past Hare and Hounds and round **L-H** bend to old Mill Bridge across River East Allen.

❷ Beyond bridge, turn **L** along tarred lane past cottages – ('to Wooley Scar'). Where track swings **R** leave it and go through gate ahead before following cross-field path, parallel to river.

❸ At narrow end of wedge-shaped field cross ladder stile on **R**. Here path veers away from river and enters area above Wooley Scar (overgrown with nettles and ragwort in summer). Route continues generally southwest across fields.

❹ Beyond Black Cleugh it swings southeast along short section of rutted track. Ignoring 1st stile on **R** follow **R** field edge. Waymark on broken fence points way towards woods surrounding Steel Burn.

❺ Turn **L** along grass track running parallel to burn and go through gate behind little cottage. Turn **R** over footbridge crossing burn, then follow banks of East Allen. Clear route crosses riverside meadows and ignores 1st river footbridge near Peckriding.

❻ After following river, path comes to track near Hagg Wood and follows it across bridge over East Allen. Track zig-zags past farm at Studdondene to B6295. Turn **L**.

❼ At woods of Parkgates Burn take **L** of 2 waymarked paths. Over stile it climbs fields towards **L** of 2 farmhouses on skyline – Low Scotch Hall. It turns **R** then **L** to round farmhouse, now following **L** field edge above valley.

❽ At woods of Prospect Hill turn **R** through animal pens then along enclosed path to farm of Finney Hill Green. Turn **L** beyond house and continue along **L** edge of 3 fields.

❾ Modern housing estate at edge of Allendale Town comes into view and path heads north, parallel to houses. In last field it descends towards more mature housing and enters estate through ginnel. Pass playground and out on to main road in village centre.

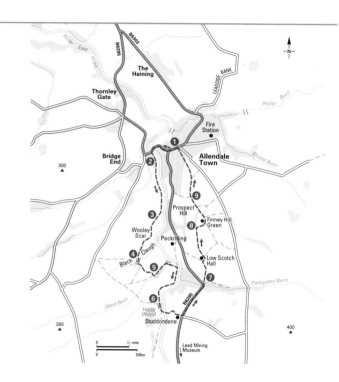

ALLENHEADS High On Byerhope Bank

Taking the high moors of Hexhamshire.

5 miles/8km 3hrs **Ascent** 656ft/200m ⚠ **Difficulty** 2
Paths Stony tracks and generally well-defined paths, 3 stiles
Map OS Explorer OL31 North Pennines **Grid ref** NY 860453
Parking In Allenheads village centre

❶ From front of heritage centre head east to B6295 and cross follow lane signposted to Rookhope. This climbs steeply from valley between spruce plantations. At sharp **L-H** bend beyond Eastend Reservoir, leave road and cross step stile on path signed 'Rookhope Road'. Trackless, but guided by wall on **R**, path climbs westwards across 2 fields of rough pasture and over 2 stiles.

❷ After cutting corner path rejoins road high on moors. Turn **L** along road for few paces, then follow stony track at **R-H** side, past quarry workings. This traces moorland rim above Allenheads, now hiding in forest.

❸ Pass quarry and huge cairn track turns **R** then meanders around Middle Rigg before turning sharp **L** to pass old ruins of Byerhope hamlet.

❹ Beyond occupied Byerhope Farm, at High Haddock Stones, track swings **R**, away from valley; here leave it. Waymarker post, first of many, highlights bridleway

wanted. This clear grooved grassy path makes circuitous descent into Allendale. After passing grassed-over quarry workings bridleway descends to gate by colourful terraced cottages on main valley road.

❺ Across road go straight on, down minor lane, which fords River East Allen; use footbridge on **R** to cross.

❻ Where road bends **R** uphill at Peasmeadows, leave it and go down cottage's drive, beyond which riverside path begins. Ignore 1st bridge across river and stay with path past Burnfoot. Cross footbridge over Middlehope Burn, then continue though pleasing little ravine of heather and bilberry. As it approaches lead mining spoil heaps path gets sketchy. Climb to brow of bank on **R** and follow this to road near Slag Hill.

❼ Turn **L** down road to recross East Allen, then turn **R** at T-junction. Lane leads back into Allenheads, past hamlet of Dirt Pot and old Presbyterian chapel.

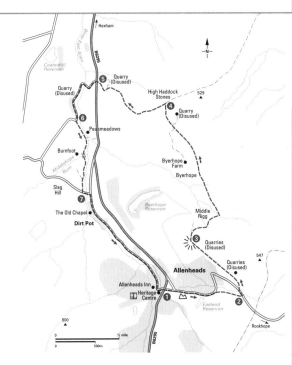

Walking in Safety

All these walks are suitable for any reasonably fit person, but less experienced walkers should try the easier walks first. Route finding is usually straightforward, but you will find that an Ordnance Survey map is a vital addition to the route maps and descriptions.

Risks

Although each walk has been researched with a view to minimising the risks to the walkers who follow its route, no walk in the countryside can be considered to be completely free from risk. Walking in the outdoors will always require a degree of common sense and judgement to ensure that it is as safe as possible.

- Be particularly careful on cliff paths and in upland terrain, where the consequences of a slip can be very serious.

- Remember to check tidal conditions before walking along the seashore.

- Some sections of route are by, or cross roads. Take care and remember traffic is a danger even on minor country lanes.

- Be careful around farmyard machinery and livestock, especially if you have children or a dog with you.

- Be aware of the consequences of changes of weather and check the forecast before you set off. Carry spare clothing and a torch if you are walking in the winter months. Remember that the weather can change very quickly at any time of the year, and in moorland and heathland areas, mist and fog can make route finding much harder. Don't set out in these conditions unless you are confident of your navigation skills in poor visibility. In summer remember to take account of the heat and sun; wear a hat and carry spare water.

- On walks away from centres of population you should carry a whistle and survival bag. If you do have an accident requiring the emergency services, make a note of your position as accurately as possible and dial 999.